Experiencing Choral Music

INTERMEDIATE

TENOR/BASS

Developed by

HAL•LEONARD®
CORPORATION

Glencoe

New York, New York   Columbus, Ohio   Chicago, Illinois   Peoria, Illinois   Woodland Hills, California

The portions of the National Standards for Music Education included here are reprinted from *National Standards for Arts Education* with permission from MENC—The National Association for Music Education. All rights reserved. Copyright © 1994 by MENC. The complete National Standards and additional materials relating to the Standards are available from MENC, 1806 Robert Fulton Drive, Reston, VA 20191 (telephone 800-336-3768).

A portion of the sales of this material goes to support music education programs through programs of MENC—The National Association for Music Education.

Glencoe

The *McGraw-Hill* Companies

Printed in the United States of America.

Send all inquiries to:
Glencoe/McGraw-Hill
21600 Oxnard Street, Suite 500
Woodland Hills, CA 91367

ISBN 0-07-861114-8 (Student Edition)
ISBN 0-07-861115-6 (Teacher Wraparound Edition)

3 4 5 6 7 8 9   045   09 08 07 06 05

134149

Credits

LEAD AUTHORS

Emily Crocker
Vice President of Choral Publications
Hal Leonard Corporation, Milwaukee, Wisconsin
Founder and Artistic Director, Milwaukee Children's Choir

Michael Jothen
Professor of Music, Program Director of Graduate Music Education
Chairperson of Music Education
Towson University, Towson, Maryland

Jan Juneau
Choral Director
Klein Collins High School
Spring, Texas

Henry H. Leck
Associate Professor and Director of Choral Activities
Butler University, Indianapolis, Indiana
Founder and Artistic Director, Indianapolis Children's Choir

Michael O'Hern
Choral Director
Lake Highlands High School
Richardson, Texas

Audrey Snyder
Composer
Eugene, Oregon

Mollie Tower
Coordinator of Choral and General Music, K-12, Retired
Austin, Texas

AUTHORS

Anne Denbow
Voice Instructor, Professional Singer/Actress
Director of Music, Holy Cross Episcopal Church
Simpsonville, South Carolina

Rollo A. Dilworth
Director of Choral Activities and Music
   Education
North Park University, Chicago, Illinois

Deidre Douglas
Choral Director
Aragon Middle School, Houston, Texas

Ruth E. Dwyer
Associate Director and Director of Education
Indianapolis Children's Choir
Indianapolis, Indiana

Norma Freeman
Choral Director
Saline High School, Saline, Michigan

Cynthia I. Gonzales
Music Theorist
Greenville, South Carolina

Michael Mendoza
Professor of Choral Activities
New Jersey State University
Trenton, New Jersey

Thomas Parente
Associate Professor
Westminster Choir College of Rider University
Princeton, New Jersey

Barry Talley
Director of Fine Arts and Choral Director
Deer Park ISD, Deer Park, Texas

CONTRIBUTING AUTHORS

Debbie Daniel
Choral Director, Webb Middle School
Garland, Texas

Roger Emerson
Composer/Arranger
Mount Shasta, California

Kari Gilbertson
Choral Director, Forest Meadow Junior High
Richardson, Texas

Tim McDonald
Creative Director, Music Theatre International
New York, New York

Christopher W. Peterson
Assistant Professor of Music Education (Choral)
University of Wisconsin-Milwaukee
Milwaukee, Wisconsin

Kirby Shaw
Composer/Arranger
Ashland, Oregon

Stephen Zegree
Professor of Music
Western Michigan State University
Kalamazoo, Michigan

EDITORIAL

Linda Rann
Senior Editor
Hal Leonard Corporation
Milwaukee, Wisconsin

Stacey Nordmeyer
Choral Editor
Hal Leonard Corporation
Milwaukee, Wisconsin

Table of Contents

Introductory Materials . . . . i–viii

Lessons

1 **This Land Is Your Land • TB** 2
Woody Guthrie, arranged by Donald Moore

Spotlight On Posture 13

2 **Be Cool • Unison Voices** 14
Bob Chilcott

Spotlight On Arranging 21

3 **Red River Valley • TB/TTB** 22
Traditional American Cowboy Song,
arranged by Emily Crocker

4 **Codfish Shanty • TB** 26
Traditional Sea Shanty, arranged by Vijay Singh

5 **Festival Procession • TB** 34
Notre Dame Conductus, arranged by Emily Crocker

6 **Soldier's Hallelujah • TB** 42
Vijay Singh

7 **Light The Candles Of Hanukkah • TB** 48
George L. O. Strid

8 **The Shepherd's Spiritual • TB** 56
American Spiritual, arranged by Donald Moore

Spotlight On Vowels 65

9 **Now Is The Month Of Maying • TTB** 66
Thomas Morley, arranged by Sherri Porterfield

10 **Der Herr segne euch • TB** 74
Johann Sebastian Bach, arranged by Barry Talley

11   **Ave Verum Corpus • TTB** 86
        Wolfgang Amadeus Mozart, arranged by Joyce Eilers

12   **Da unten im Tale • TB** 94
        Johannes Brahms, arranged by Barry Talley

Music & History

Renaissance Period 99

Baroque Period 100

Classical Period 104

Romantic Period 112

Contemporary Period 116

Spotlight On Diction 120

Choral Library

The Battle Cry Of Freedom • TB 122
        George Frederick Root, arranged by Patti DeWitt

Spotlight On Careers In Music 127

Come Travel With Me • TTB 128
        Scott Farthing

Spotlight On Concert Etiquette 139

Frog Went A-Courtin' • TB 140
        Traditional Folk Song, arranged by Audrey Snyder

Guantanamera • TB 152
        Cuban Folk Song, arranged by John Higgins

Joshua! (Fit The Battle Of Jericho) • TTB 158
Traditional Spiritual, arranged by Kirby Shaw

Spotlight On Breath Management 169

Leave Her, Johnny • TB/TTB 170
Traditional Sea Chantey, arranged by Emily Crocker

New River Train • TB 174
American Spiritual, arranged by Donald Moore

Spotlight On Improvisation 183

On The Deep, Blue Sea • TTB 184
Mary Donnelly, arranged by George L.O. Strid

Spotlight On Changing Voice 197

Pretty Saro • TTB 198
American Folk Song, arranged by Jennifer B. Scoggin

Santa Lucia • TB 206
Teodoro Cottrau, arranged by Henry Leck

Sing To The Lord • TTB 212
Emily Crocker

Spotlight On Vocal Production 217

You Gentlemen Of England • TB 218
Time of Elizabeth, arranged by Barry Talley

Glossary 225

Classified Index 239

Index of Songs and Spotlights 241

TO THE STUDENT

Welcome to choir!

By singing in the choir, you have chosen to be a part of an exciting and rewarding adventure. The benefits of being in choir are many. Basically, singing is fun. It provides an expressive way of sharing your feelings and emotions. Through choir, you will have friends that share a common interest with you. You will experience the joy of making beautiful music together. Choir provides the opportunity to develop your interpersonal skills. It takes teamwork and cooperation to sing together, and you must learn how to work with others. As you critique your individual and group performances, you can improve your ability to analyze and communicate your thoughts clearly.

Even if your do not pursue a music career, music can be an important part of your life. There are many avocational opportunities in music. **Avocational** means *not related to a job or career*. Singing as a hobby can provide you with personal enjoyment, enrich your life, and teach you life skills. Singing is something you can do for the rest of your life.

In this course, you will be presented with the basic skills of vocal production and music literacy. You will be exposed to songs from different cultures, songs in many different styles and languages, and songs from various historical periods. You will discover connections between music and the other arts. Guidelines for becoming a better singer and choir member include:

- Come to class prepared to learn.
- Respect the efforts of others.
- Work daily to improve your sight-singing skills.
- Sing expressively at all times.
- Have fun singing.

This book was written to provide you with a meaningful choral experience. Take advantage of the knowledge and opportunities offered here. Your exciting adventure of experiencing choral music is about to begin!

Lessons

Lessons for the Beginning of the Year

1   This Land Is Your Land 2

2   Be Cool 14

3   Red River Valley 22

4   Codfish Shanty 26

Lessons for Mid-Winter

5   Festival Procession 34

6   Soldier's Hallelujah 42

7   Light The Candles Of Hanukkah 48

8   The Shepherd's Spiritual 56

Lessons for Concert/Festival

9   Now Is The Month Of Maying 66

10 Der Herr segne euch 74

11 Ave Verum Corpus 86

12 Da unten im Tale 94

This Land Is Your Land

Composer: Woody Guthrie, arranged by Donald Moore
Text: Woody Guthrie
Voicing: TB

VOCABULARY

arrangement

major tonality

cut time

Focus

- Sing a melody expressively in G major tonality.
- Read and perform rhythmic patterns in cut time.
- Perform music representing American heritage.

SPOTLIGHT

To learn more about arranging, see page 21.

Getting Started

Here are some of America's spectacular natural wonders. In which states are they located?

The Grand Canyon	The Great Smoky Mountains
The Everglades	Mount McKinley
Old Faithful	Niagara Falls

"This Land Is Your Land" is a tribute to the natural beauty of America. It's easy to show your pride, admiration and appreciation of our country as you perform this popular song.

◆ History and Culture

Woody Guthrie (1912–1967), who composed "This Land Is Your Land" in 1940, is considered one of the most influential songwriters of the twentieth century. He wrote songs about what he saw and experienced as he traveled across America from the 1930s to the 1950s. Besides writing prose, poetry and children's songs, Guthrie wrote songs of social, political and spiritual justice and injustice. Born in Oklahoma, he spent much of his adult life in California and New York.

"This Land Is Your Land" is an example of a choral **arrangement,** or *a piece of music in which a composer takes an existing song and adds extra features or makes changes in some way.* Contemporary composer Donald Moore uses several phrases of "America The Beautiful" to complement Guthrie's original melody.

Links to Learning

◆ Vocal

Perform the following example to establish G **major tonality** (*a song that is based on a major scale with* do *as its keynote, or hometone*). Can you feel the G major tonality and the notes leading you to the pitch *do*?

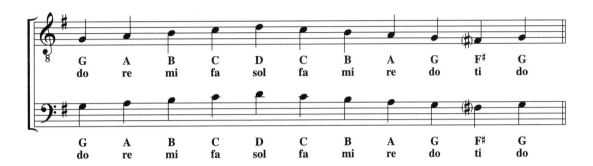

G	A	B	C	D	C	B	A	G	F♯	G
do	re	mi	fa	sol	fa	mi	re	do	ti	do

G	A	B	C	D	C	B	A	G	F♯	G
do	re	mi	fa	sol	fa	mi	re	do	ti	do

◆ Theory

This arrangement is written in **cut time (¢),** or *the time signature in which there are two beats per measure and the half note receives the beat.* Perform the following example by having one group chant the steady beat "1, 2, 1, 2," while the other group claps the rhythm. Switch roles.

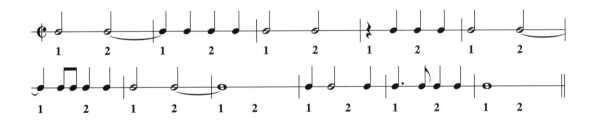

Evaluation

Demonstrate how well you have learned the skills and concepts featured in the lesson "This Land Is Your Land."

- Sing your voice part expressively in measures 4–11 on the correct solfège syllables. Ask a classmate to check for accuracy.

- With one singer on each part, chant the words in rhythm in measures 69–85, keeping a steady beat in cut time. How well did you do?

This Land Is Your Land

For TB and Piano

Arranged by
DONALD MOORE (ASCAP)

Words and Music by WOODY GUTHRIE (1912–1967)
Quoting America The Beautiful
Music by SAMUEL WARD (1848–1903)
Words by KATHARINE LEE BATES (1859–1929)

walk - ing_____ that rib - bon of high - way, I saw a -
(2.) shin - ing_____ and I was stroll - ing and the wheat fields

walk - ing_____ that rib - bon of high - way, I saw a -
(2.) shin - ing_____ and I was stroll - ing and the wheat fields

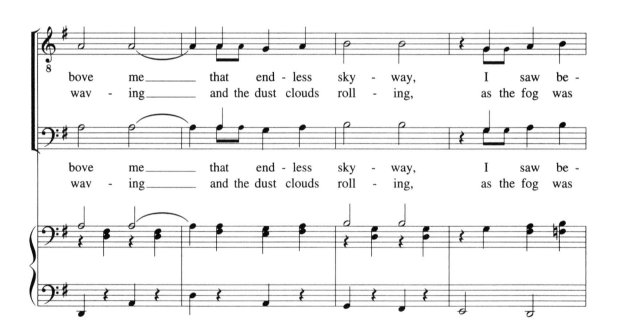

bove me_____ that end - less sky - way, I saw be -
wav - ing_____ and the dust clouds roll - ing, as the fog was

bove me_____ that end - less sky - way, I saw be -
wav - ing_____ and the dust clouds roll - ing, as the fog was

 **SPOTLIGHT**

Posture

Posture is important for good singing. By having the body properly aligned, you are able to breathe correctly so that you have sufficient breath support needed to sing more expressively and for longer periods of time.

To experience, explore and establish proper posture for singing, try the following:

Standing

- Pretend someone is gently pulling up on a thread attached to the top of your head.

- Let out all of your air like a deflating balloon.

- Raise your arms up over your head.

- Take in a deep breath as if you were sipping through a straw.

- Slowly lower your arms down to your sides.

- Let all your air out on a breathy "pah," keeping your chest high.

- Both feet on floor, shoulder-width apart.

- Chest high, shoulders relaxed.

- Neck relaxed, head straight.

Sitting

- Sit on the edge of a chair with your feet flat on the floor while keeping your chest lifted.

- Hold your music with one hand and turn pages with the other.

- Always hold the music up so you can easily see the director and your music.

Be Cool

Composer: Bob Chilcott (b. 1955)
Text: Bob Chilcott
Voicing: Unison

VOCABULARY

Jazz

Contemporary period

accidental

flat

natural

MUSIC & HISTORY

To learn more about the Contemporary period, see page 116.

Focus

- Identify and perform musical symbols (accidentals) found in music.
- Identify and perform swing-style rhythms.
- Perform music representing cool jazz style.

Getting Started

- In the past one hundred years, the earth has warmed by 1°F. Scientists predict that the average global temperature may increase by 2–6°F over the next hundred years.

This is not cool!

- Little changes in the climate can result in big changes for all people on Earth. These changes can affect the level of the oceans, the land we use for crops, the air we breathe and the water we drink.

This is not cool!

- We can make big differences in little ways! We can turn off the lights and save electricity. We can recycle bottles and cans. We can plant trees. We can ride our bikes or walk.

Now this is cool!

◆ History and Culture

The song "Be Cool" is a cool way to remind your audience about global warming. **Jazz** is *a popular style of music characterized by strong meter, improvisation and syncopated rhythms* that was developed during the **Contemporary period** *(1900–present)*. Cool jazz emerged in the 1950s as a reaction to a complex, improvised jazz style of the 1940s called bebop. "Be Cool" is written in a cool jazz style that uses a less complicated melody and rhythm than bebop. You will astound your audience with your cool sounds of vocal jazz.

Now this is cool!

Links to Learning

◆ Vocal

An **accidental** is *any sharp, flat or natural that is not included in the key signature of the piece.* A **flat** (♭) is *a symbol that lowers the pitch of a given note one half step,* and a **natural** (♮) is *a symbol that cancels a previous sharp or flat.* Read and perform the following example to hear and sing the difference between *mi* and *me.*

do mi mi   me me me   do me me   mi mi do

◆ Artistic Expression

Perform "Be Cool" in a cool jazz style by treating the dotted rhythmic patterns like a swing triplet. To prepare to do this, first chant the traditional triplet pattern (example 1). Then, chant the swing eighth pattern (example 2). Finally, the dotted eighth and sixteenth note patterns found in "Be Cool" should be performed in the swing eighth pattern (example 3).

1 Traditional Eighth Note Triplets

tri - o - la tri - o - la tri - o - la tri - o - la   tri - o - la tri - o - la tri - o - la tri - o - la

2 Swing Eighth Note Pattern

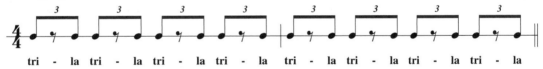

tri - la tri - la tri - la tri - la   tri - la tri - la tri - la tri - la

3 Swing Dotted Eighth Note Pattern

tri - la tri - la tri - la tri - la   tri - la tri - la tri - la tri - la

Evaluation

Demonstrate how well you have learned the skills and concepts featured in the lesson "Be Cool" by completing the following:

- Locate three examples of accidentals in the music. How did they alter the pitch?

- Sing measures 4–19 to demonstrate the difference between the pitches *mi* and *me*. Can you sing both pitches in tune?

- Perform measures 21–22 to demonstrate your ability to sing swing-style rhythms. Evaluate how well you did.

Be Cool

from *Green Songs*

For Unison Voices and Piano

Words and Music by
BOB CHILCOTT

OXFORD UNIVERSITY PRESS, MUSIC DEPARTMENT, GREAT CLARENDON STREET, OXFORD OX2 6DP
Photocopying this copyright material is ILLEGAL.

SPOTLIGHT

Arranging

In music, an **arrangement** is *a composition in which a composer takes an existing melody and adds extra features or changes the melody in some way.* An **arranger** is *a composer who writes an arrangement by changing an existing melody to fit certain musical parameters.* The arranger has the following things to consider:

- Pitch—What is the range of the melody?
- Tempo—What is the speed of the beat?
- Instrumentation—Is the music for voices, instruments or both?
- Accompaniment—What will be used for accompaniment (piano, guitar, etc.), if anything?
- Harmony—What type of chords will be used for the harmony?
- Melody/Countermelody—Will harmony be added by use of a **countermelody** *(a separate vocal line that supports and contrasts the primary melody)*?

Read and perform the familiar melody "Hot Cross Buns."

Hot cross buns,   hot cross buns.   One a pen-ny, two a pen-ny,   hot cross buns.

Now you are ready to write your own arrangement. Using "Hot Cross Buns" as the existing melody, decide which element or elements you wish to change to compose your arrangement. You can try one or more of the ideas listed below:

- Pitch—Start the song higher or lower than currently written.
- Tempo—Alter the tempo in some manner (faster or slower).
- Instrumentation—Play the melody on different instruments.
- Accompaniment—Use a piano, guitar or other instrument to accompany your melody.
- Harmony—Add harmony notes from the chords and play them on an instrument or sing them with the melody.
- Melody/Countermelody—Compose a second melody or countermelody that fits musically with the existing melody.

Red River Valley

Composer: Traditional American Cowboy Song, arranged by Emily Crocker
Text: Traditional
Voicing: TB/TTB

 **SPOTLIGHT**

To learn more about the changing voice, see page 195.

Focus

- Sing a cappella music in three-part harmony.
- Use dynamics to sing expressively.
- Perform music representing American heritage.

Getting Started

When you hear the words "Once upon a time," you know a story is about to be told. The storyteller often adds vocal inflection, facial expression and an occasional hand gesture to make the story appealing to the listener. As a singer, you must make your song appealing to the listener. You can raise the quality of your performance through enhanced facial expression, proper vocal production and good **stage presence** *(one's overall appearance on stage).*

◆ History and Culture

A **folk song** is *a song that was originally passed down from generation to generation through oral tradition and often describes a certain place or event.* The folk song "The Red River Valley," so popular with the American cowboy, is based on a nineteenth-century tune "In the Bright Mohawk Valley."

During the late 1800s, cattle drives from Texas to Kansas were important in the American Southwest. Texas cowboys could get a higher price for their cattle in Kansas than they could in Texas. The large cattle drives would take several months to reach their final destination. The Red River, forming the Oklahoma and Texas border, served as one of the markers along the way. Stampedes, changing weather, disease and river crossings often made life dangerous on the trail. But in the evenings gathered around a campfire, the cowboys would sing songs of adventure, humor and love.

Dynamics *(symbols in music that indicate how loud or soft to sing)* can change the character of a song or give it expressiveness. After you have learned "Red River Valley," experiment with different dynamic markings to create another interpretation of the song.

Links to Learning

◆ Vocal

The **melody** (*a logical succession of musical tones*) is usually very prominent in folk songs. However, in this arrangement, the melody moves from line to line. To hear the complete melody, sing the following example in a comfortable range for your voice.

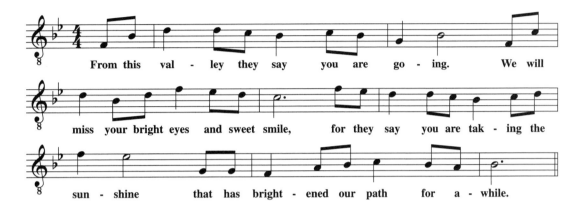

From this val - ley they say you are go - ing. We will

miss your bright eyes and sweet smile, for they say you are tak - ing the

sun - shine that has bright - ened our path for a - while.

◆ Theory

A **chord** is *a combination of three or more notes sung together at the same time.* The harmony in "Red River Valley" is created when the three voice parts move from chord to chord. Perform the following example to practice singing chords.

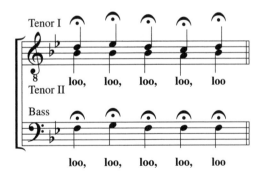

Tenor I

Tenor II

loo, loo, loo, loo, loo

Bass

loo, loo, loo, loo, loo

Evaluation

Demonstrate how well you have learned the skills and concepts featured in the lesson "Red River Valley" by completing the following:

- In a trio with one singer on each part, perform measures 1–8. Evaluate how well you were able to sing a cappella in three-part harmony.

- Sing measures 9–18 alone or with others to show how you can express the meaning of the text through your stage presence and use of dynamics. How well did you do?

Red River Valley

For TB or TTB, a cappella

Arranged by
EMILY CROCKER

Traditional American Cowboy Song

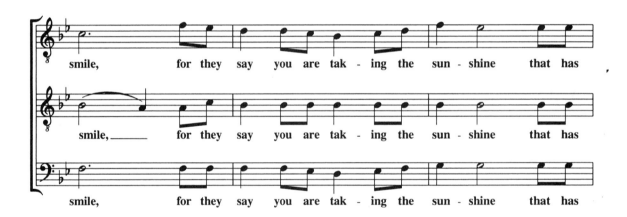

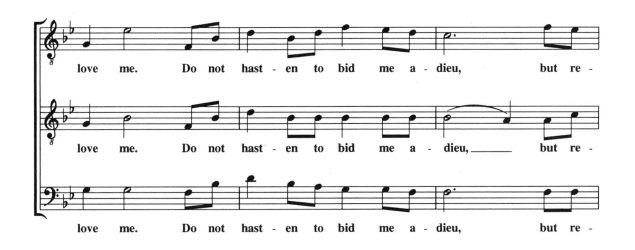

love me. Do not hast-en to bid me a-dieu, but re-

mem-ber the Red Riv-er Val-ley, and the cow-boy who loved you so

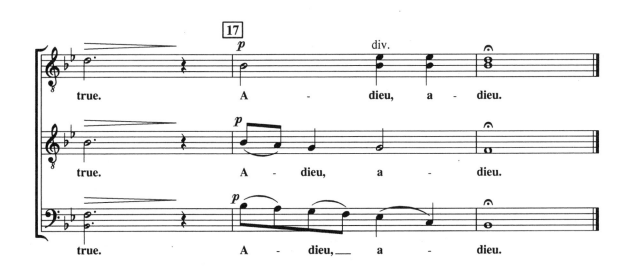

true. A - dieu, a - dieu.

134149

Codfish Shanty

Composer: Traditional, arranged by Vijay Singh
Text: Traditional Sea Chantey
Voicing: TB

VOCABULARY

sea chantey

articulation

staccato

accent

Focus

- Define *staccato* and *accent*. Perform music that contains both.
- Read and perform dotted eighth and sixteenth note patterns.
- Perform music representing the sea chantey.

Getting Started

When it comes to cleaning your room at home, which description best fits you?

1. You love to clean and go right to work.

2. You do not enjoy cleaning, but if you play music or sing, the work gets done.

If you relate to the second statement, you have something in common with eighteenth-century sailors. "Codfish Shanty" is a **sea chantey,** or *a song sung by sailors in the rhythm of their work.* When you notice that the word *chantey* was transformed into *shanty*, you will not be surprised to learn that there are many different versions of this song.

 **SPOTLIGHT**

To learn more about careers in music, see page 125.

◆ History and Culture

The work aboard early sailing ships included pulling the ropes, hoisting the sails and raising the anchor. The work was often repetitive and took a long time to complete. Sometimes the sailors created upbeat chanteys to pass the time that included improvised, humorous verses. This was probably the case with "Codfish Shanty." The various versions of this song refer to different towns and different situations. Every version, however, pokes fun in a good-natured way at the home ports of the sailors. After you learn this song, you might want to sing it while you clean your room.

Arranger Vijay Singh is a teacher and composer at Central Washington University, where he directs the University Choir and heads the vocal jazz program.

Links to Learning

◆ Vocal

Articulation *(the amount of separation or connection between notes)* is used in music to show a singer how to sing the notes. A **staccato** marking (♪) is *a symbol that indicates to sing a note short and detached.* An **accent** (♪) is *a symbol that indicates that a note should receive extra emphasis or stress.* Perform the following example to demonstrate your understanding of staccato and accent markings.

◆ Theory

Read and perform the following rhythmic patterns, making sure there is a clear distinction between the groupings of two eighth notes and groupings of dotted eighth and sixteenth notes.

◆ Artistic Expression

To show artistry through performance practices, chant the words of "Codfish Shanty" from measures 8–24. Use facial expression, vocal inflections, and other gestures to emphasize the text. Use these expressions when performing the piece.

Evaluation

Demonstrate how well you have learned the skills and concepts featured in the lesson "Codfish Shanty" by completing the following:

- Define *staccato* and *accent*. Identify these articulation markings in the music and perform them appropriately. Evaluate how well you were able to perform them differently.

- Compose a four-measure rhythmic pattern in $\frac{2}{4}$ meter using eighth notes and dotted eighth and sixteenth note combinations. Perform your composition on a rhythm instrument for another student. Check each other's work for rhythmic accuracy.

Codfish Shanty

TB and Piano

Arranged by
VIJAY SINGH (ASCAP)

Traditional

Oh, Glos' - ter girls they have no combs.

Oh, Glos' - ter girls they have no combs.

don't you make a noise? We're bound for South Aus - tra - lia!

don't you make a noise? We're bound for South Aus - tra - lia!

Oh, Glos' - ter boys they have no sleds.

Heave a - way, heave a - way! They slide down hills on

Heave a - way, heave a - way!

Festival Procession

Composer: Emily Crocker
Text: Anonymous Latin Text, English text by Emily Crocker
Voicing: TB

VOCABULARY

conductus

mode

Mixolydian scale

$\frac{6}{4}$ meter

Focus

- Identify and perform music in a modal key (Mixolydian).
- Read and perform music in $\frac{6}{4}$ meter.
- Create an original percussion arrangement.

 **SKILL BUILDERS**

To learn more about modes and modal scales, see Intermediate Sight-Singing, *page 168.*

Getting Started

Have you ever been in a processional? You may have seen a processional at a school graduation as the graduates filed into the auditorium, or at a wedding as the bridal party walked down the aisle. "Festival Procession" is a musical processional intended to be sung at the beginning of a concert. Composer Emily Crocker suggests using banners, percussion or other instruments as you sing and walk to make your processional festive.

◆ History and Culture

You only have to learn the first four measures of "Festival Procession" to discover that the song has a very distinctive sound. This is because Emily Crocker has set words from a medieval Latin text to music adapted from a **conductus,** or *a thirteenth-century song for two, three or four voices.* "Festival Procession" is in two parts. Because there is not a third note in each chord, the resulting harmony has an open and hollow sound. When you tune your notes carefully and sing with rhythmic precision, your processional will be very dramatic even if you are standing still.

The English translation of the Latin text is:

Novus annus hodie monet nos letitie laudes inchoare.

Today a new year urges us joyful praises to begin.

Eya rex nos adiuva qui gubernas omnia.

Ah! King, help us, who governs all.

Links to Learning

◆ **Vocal**

A **mode** is *an early system of pitch organization that was used before major and minor keys were developed.* The **Mixolydian scale** is *a modal scale that follows the pattern of* sol *to* sol. "Festival Procession" is based on the G Mixolydian scale and uses the notes G, A, B, C, D, E F, G. To locate "G" on the piano, find any set of three black keys. "G" is the white key just to the left of the middle black key. Using the keyboard below as a guide, play the G Mixolydian scale.

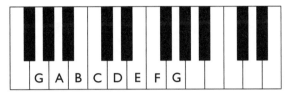

The G major scale is similar to the G Mixolydian scale. The G major scale uses an F♯ *(ti)*; however, in the G Mixolydian mode, the F♯ *(ti)* is lowered to F natural *(te)*. Perform the following examples to compare the G major and G Mixolydian scales.

◆ **Theory**

"Festival Procession" is written in $\frac{6}{4}$ **meter,** *a meter in which there are two groups of three quarter notes per measure and the dotted half note receives the beat.* Read and clap the following example to practice rhythmic patterns in $\frac{6}{4}$ meter.

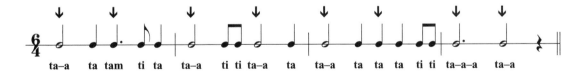

Evaluation

Demonstrate how well you have learned the skills and concepts featured in the lesson "Festival Procession" by completing the following:

- In a small group, sing measures 26–33 to show that you can sing in tune in a modal tonality. Evaluate how well you were able to sing in tune.

- Using what you have learned about $\frac{6}{4}$ meter, write an original percussion arrangement that can be played as you sing "Festival Procession." Check your work for rhythmic accuracy.

For the Haltom High School Men's Chorus
Fort Worth, Texas
1996 TMEA Honor Choir
Stuart Younse, Director

Festival Procession

For TB, a cappella with Optional Percussion

Anonymous Latin Text (Munich clm 20153)
English Lyrics by EMILY CROCKER

Notre Dame Conductus
(Music adapted from 13th Century)
Arranged by EMILY CROCKER

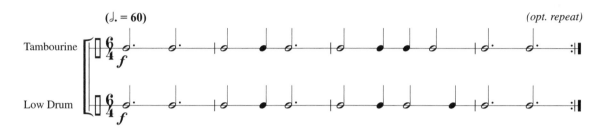

Percussion part found at end of song.

No - vus an - nus ho - di - e_____ mon - et nos le - ti - ti - e

lau - des in - cho - a - re. E - ya rex_____ nos a - diu - va,

E - ya rex nos a - diu - va qui gu - ber - nas_____ om - ni - a.

Joy - ful, joy - ful sing we all_____ on this hap - py_____

morn - ing. Play the drum,_____ come ye all,_____ join us in_____ our_____

sing - ing. Why this hap - py ju - bi - lee with

Festival Procession

Anonymous Latin Text (Munich clm 20153)
English Lyrics by EMILY CROCKER

Notre Dame Conductus
(Music adapted from 13th Century)
Arranged by EMILY CROCKER

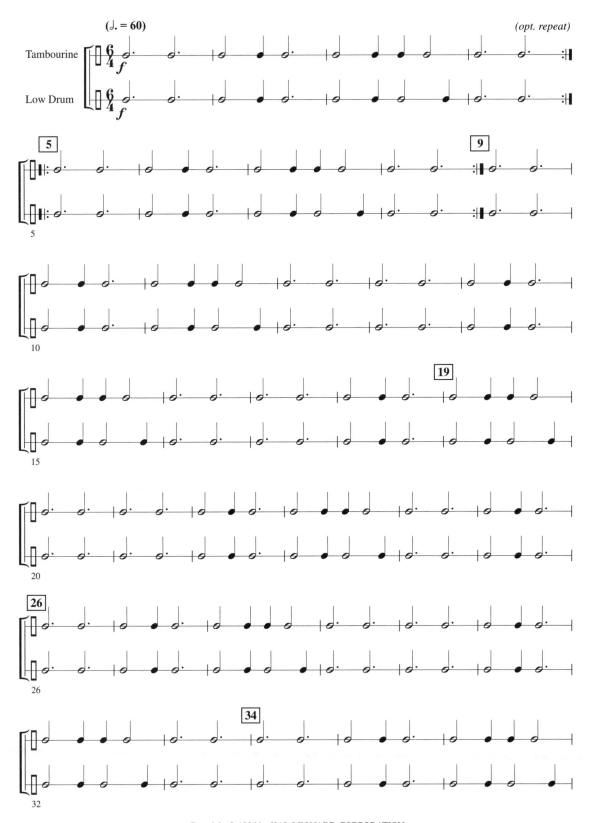

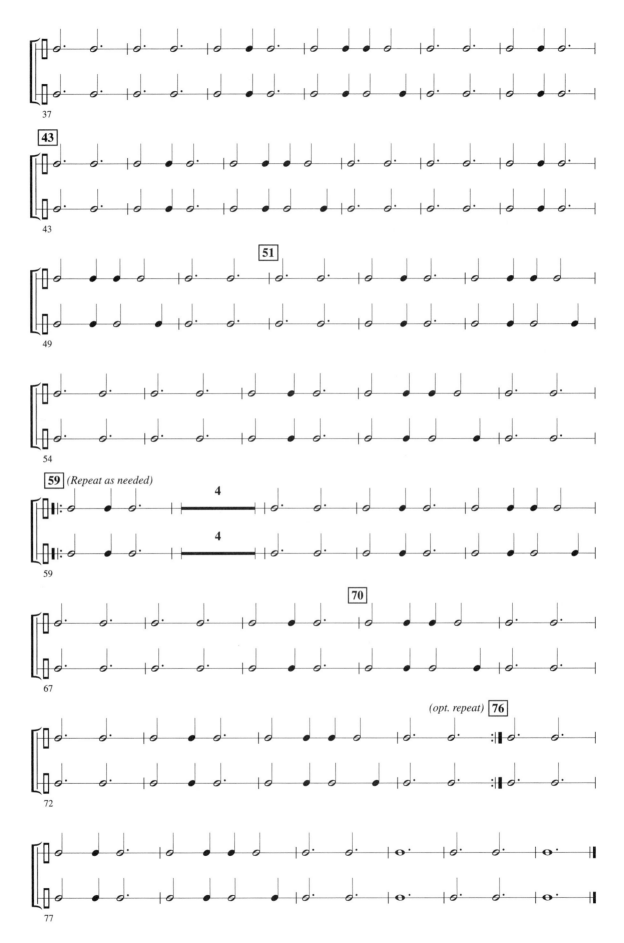

Soldier's Hallelujah

Composer: Vijay Singh
Text: Vijay Singh
Voicing: TB

VOCABULARY

form

phrase

coda

accidental

dynamics

 **SKILL BUILDERS**

To learn more about accidentals, see Intermediate Sight-Singing, *page 156 and 157.*

Focus

- Identify and describe form in music.
- Interpret dynamics when performing.
- Perform a cappella music in two parts.

Getting Started

If you presently sing in a male choir, you have joined a very prestigious and historical choral tradition. Male choirs can trace their origins to the early medieval days of the church. Throughout history, male choirs have played significant roles in many cultures and countries. For instance, the Vienna Boys Choir and boarding school have been musical fixtures in Vienna, Austria, for over 500 years. In addition, every small mining town in Wales seemed to have a thriving male chorus made up of community members and miners at the beginning of the twentieth century. And today in America, many cities support boys' choirs that are patterned after their European counterparts. Given all this male singing history, a song called "Soldier's Hallelujah" seems quite natural.

◆ History and Culture

Form *(the design and structure of a composition)* is as important in music as it is in visual art. Without an organized form, a piece of music cannot present a cohesive musical idea. The American composer Vijay Singh wrote "Soldier's Hallelujah" in nine 4-measure **phrases** *(musical ideas with a beginning and an end)* and a **coda** *(a concluding portion of a composition)*. Singh's three principal melodies, introduced in measures 1, 9 and 25, define the three contrasting phrases of the piece and are called sections A, B and C. In what order does Singh use sections A, B and C for the nine phrases?

Links to Learning

◆ Vocal

An **accidental** is *any sharp, flat or natural sign that is not included in the key signature of a piece of music.* When singing "Soldier's Hallelujah," both voice parts must use *fi* instead of *fa* in sections A and B. Sing the following examples, first with *fa* and then with *fi*, to become familiar with the altered sound. Find these examples in the music.

◆ Theory

To analyze the form of this song, identify and label the nine sections and coda found in "Soldier's Hallelujah." You will discover that section A appears six times. Describe how Singh varied each repetition.

◆ Artistic Expression

Dynamics are *symbols in music used to indicate how loud or soft to sing a passage.* Review measures 29–40 in the music. Since the only word used is "Hallelujah," it is the changes in dynamics that create the artistic shape of this section. Locate the dynamic markings *mp* (medium soft), *f* (loud), *sub. p* (suddenly soft), *molto cresc.* (gradually getting louder), and *ff* (very loud). Observe these dynamic markings.

Evaluation

Demonstrate how well you have learned the skills and concepts featured in the lesson "Soldier's Hallelujah" by completing the following:

- Using visual arts (drawing, painting, sculpture, graph, etc.), design a piece of artwork that represents the form of "Soldier's Hallelujah." Show each variation of section A in a different manner. Share your work with the class. Critique how well the artwork represents the music.

- Record yourself singing measures 29–40 into a microphone. Listen to the recording and evaluate how well you were able to perform the dynamic markings indicated.

Soldier's Hallelujah

For TB, a cappella, with Optional Snare and Tenor Drum

**Words and Music by
VIJAY SINGH**

Optional Snare and Tenor Drum ostinato (continues throughout). Ostinato may begin four measures before voices enter; drums at last measure of piece should play the rhythm of the baritone melody.

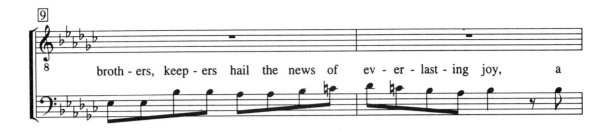

broth - ers, keep - ers hail the news of ev - er - last - ing joy, a

King is born to save us all, re - joice, the might - y boy! Hal - le -

lu! Hal - le - lu - jah!
Hal - le - lu - jah, hal - le - lu - jah, hal - le - lu, hal - le - lu - jah!

Hal - le - lu - jah, hal - le - lu - jah, hal - le - lu - jah! We

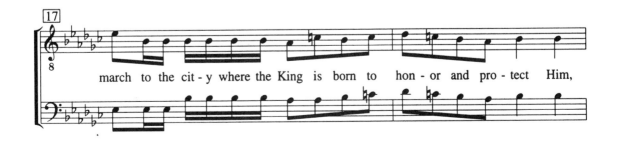

march to the cit - y where the King is born to hon - or and pro - tect Him,

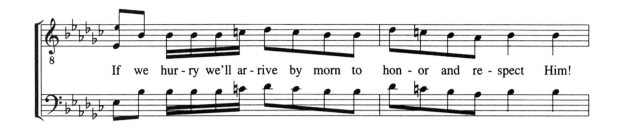

If we hur-ry we'll ar-rive by morn to hon-or and re-spect Him!

[21] *mp*

Hal - le - lu - jah, hal - le - lu - jah, hal - le - lu, hal - le - lu - jah!

mf

Hal - le - lu - jah, hal - le - lu - jah, hal - le - lu - jah! All

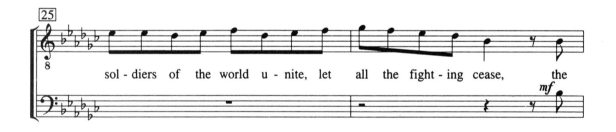

[25]

sol - diers of the world u - nite, let all the fight - ing cease, the

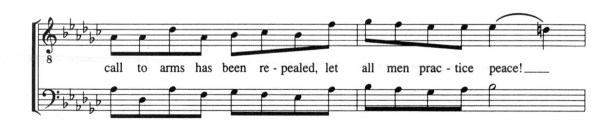

call to arms has been re - pealed, let all men prac - tice peace!___

Light The Candles Of Hanukkah

Composer: George L. O. Strid
Text: Mary Donnelly
Voicing: TB

VOCABULARY

breath support

harmonic minor scale

relative minor scale

Focus

- Distinguish between major and minor tonality.
- Sing with adequate support.
- Perform music representing the Jewish culture.

Getting Started

Holidays are a time for family traditions, unique foods and no school! Holidays often include special music. For instance, what holiday goes with each of these famous tunes?

1. "America the Beautiful"
2. "Auld Lang Syne"
3. "Deck The Halls"
4. "Ma'oz Tzur"

If you had difficulty in identifying the last one, it's because the song and holiday are not quite as well known as the others. "Ma'oz Tzur" ("Rock of Ages") is sung during Hanukkah, the Jewish festival of lights. Hanukkah begins on the Hebrew date of the 25th of Kislev and lasts for eight days in late November or December.

◆ History and Culture

Hanukkah means "dedication" and commemorates the victory of the outnumbered Maccabees (led by Judah) over a much larger army of Syrian Greeks (led by King Antiochus IV) in 165 B.C. The victory was considered a miracle. But once the temple in Jerusalem had been reclaimed, it had to be rededicated. According to legend, only one jar of sacramental oil was found, enough to light a flame for only one day. Miraculously, the oil burned for eight days, thus the eight days of Hanukkah.

Although not a traditional song, "Light The Candles Of Hanukkah" has a holiday tune that you may find yourself humming all year long.

 **SPOTLIGHT**

To learn more about breath management, see page 167.

Links to Learning

◆ Vocal

When you perform the following example, you must maintain adequate **breath support** *(a constant airflow necessary to produce sound for singing)* to sing one word for two notes. Practice singing very smoothly with lots of breath support so there is no "H" sound when you change pitches.

◆ Theory

"Light The Candles Of Hanukkah" uses major and minor scales. Read and perform the B♭ major scale and G **harmonic minor scale** *(a minor scale that uses a raised seventh note; si is raised from sol)*. G minor is called the **relative minor scale** to B♭ major because it is *a minor scale that shares the same key signature as its corresponding major scale.* Sing in your appropriate octave or range. When the notes feel high, change to your **falsetto** voice *(the light upper range of male singers).*

Evaluation

Demonstrate how well you have learned the skills and concepts featured in the lesson "Light The Candles Of Hanukkah" by completing the following:

- Play the "major/minor" game with a friend. Sing example 1 or example 2 from the Theory section above on a neutral syllable. Ask a friend to identify if you are singing a major or minor scale. Switch roles. How well did you do?

- Sing your voice part in measures 38–45. Evaluate how well you are able to sing with adequate breath support and not allow any "H" sounds to occur between the notes.

Light The Candles Of Hanukkah

For TB and Piano

Words by
MARY DONNELLY (ASCAP)

Music by
GEORGE L. O. STRID (ASCAP)

Ha - nuk - kah! Let the drei - dels__ spin.

Ha - nuk - kah! Let the drei - dels spin.

We're so glad that it's Ha - nuk - kah. Let the fun be -

We're so glad that it's Ha - nuk - kah. Let the fun be -

gin! Now we ga - ther,

gin! Now we ga - ther,

The Shepherd's Spiritual

Composer: American Spiritual, arranged by Donald Moore
Text: Traditional
Voicing: TB

VOCABULARY

spiritual

call and response

solo

altered pitch

quartet

 **SKILL BUILDERS**

To learn more about syncopation, see Intermediate Sight-Singing, *page 126.*

Focus

- Perform expressively in both solo and ensemble singing.
- Read and perform rhythmic patterns that contain syncopation.
- Perform music representing the African American spiritual.

Getting Started

What makes a song fun to sing? Think of your favorite song. Why is the song appealing to you? On a sheet of paper, make a list of factors that contribute to making a song fun to sing. Share your list with the class.

As you learn "The Shepherd's Spiritual," look for features in the song that appear on your list. These might include (1) a singable melody, (2) catchy rhythms, (3) an inspirational text, (4) variety in texture (many voices versus a few voices), and (5) an opportunity to sing a solo. Among the many reasons to sing a song, having fun is one of the most important.

◆ History and Culture

"The Shepherd's Spiritual" is actually an arrangement of the holiday spiritual "Rise Up, Shepherd, and Follow." A part of the African American tradition, a **spiritual** is *a song that was first sung by slaves and is often based on a biblical theme or story.* Spirituals were probably sung while the slaves were working in the fields, engaging in social activities, or participating in worship. The use of syncopation and complex rhythms is very often found in spirituals.

This arrangement features **call and response,** *a technique in which a leader or group sings a phrase (call) followed by a response of the same phrase or a continuation of the phrase by another group.* This technique was often used in the creation and teaching of spirituals. It is found in the verses of this arrangement, and the call may be performed as a **solo** *(one person singing alone).*

Links to Learning

◆ Vocal

An **altered pitch** is the same as an accidental, or *any pitch that is changed by a sharp, flat or natural that is not included in the key signature of the piece.* Altered pitches are used in "The Shepherd's Spiritual" when F♯ (*mi*) changes to F♮ (*me*—pronounced "meh" or "mā"). Perform the following example to practice tuning altered pitches. Sing in the range that best fits your voice.

do   do la do   do do   me re do do___   mi mi re do la   do   do___

◆ Theory

Read and perform the following example to practice the syncopated rhythms used in this song. Divide into two groups. Chant and clap the lines separately and then together.

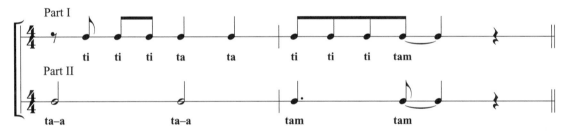

ti   ti ti ta   ta   ti   ti ti tam

ta–a   ta–a   tam   tam

Evaluation

Demonstrate how well you have learned the skills and concepts featured in the lesson "The Shepherd's Spiritual" by completing the following:

- Form a **quartet** *(a group of four singers)*. Sing measures 4–12 taking turns singing the solo lines. Evaluate your performance based on in-tune singing, rhythmic accuracy and musical expression.

- With a partner, take turns singing measures 24–32 while the other claps or taps beats 2 and 4. Evaluate how well you were able to sing syncopation accurately and maintain the steady beat.

The Shepherd's Spiritual

For TB and Piano

Arranged with additional music by
DONALD MOORE

Based on an American Spiritual

With drive (♩ = 122)

Tambourine

mf cresc.

solo or unison

There's a star in the East on Christ-mas morn,___

SPOTLIGHT

Vowels

The style of a given piece of music dictates how we should pronounce the words. If we are singing a more formal, classical piece, then we need to form taller vowels as in very proper English. If we are singing in a jazz or pop style, then we should pronounce the words in a more relaxed, conversational way. To get the feeling of taller vowels for classical singing, do the following:

- Let your jaw gently drop down and back as if it were on a hinge.
- Place your hands on your cheeks beside the corners of your mouth.
- Sigh on an *ah* [ɑ] vowel sound, but do not spread the corners of your mouth.
- Now sigh on other vowel sounds—*eh* [ɛ], *ee* [i], *oh* [o] and *oo* [u]—keeping the back of the tongue relaxed.
- As your voice goes from higher notes to lower notes, think of gently opening a tiny umbrella inside your mouth.

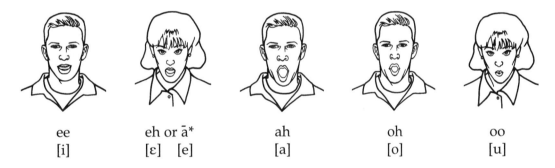

ee	eh or ā*	ah	oh	oo
[i]	[ɛ] [e]	[a]	[o]	[u]

Other vowel sounds used in singing are diphthongs. A **diphthong** is *a combination of two vowel sounds*. For example, the vowel *ay* consists of two sounds: *eh* [E] and *ee* [i]. To sing a diphthong correctly, stay on the first vowel sound for the entire length of the note, only lightly adding the second vowel sound as you move to another note or lift off the note.

I = *ah*_____(ee) [ɑi]

boy = *oh*_____(ee) [oi]

down = *ah*_____(oo) [ɑu]

*Note: This is an Italian "ā," which is one sound, and not an American "ā," which is a diphthong, or two sounds.

Now Is The Month of Maying

Composer: Thomas Morley (1557–1602), arranged by Sherri Porterfield
Text: Thomas Morley
Voicing: TTB

VOCABULARY

Renaissance period

madrigal

homophony

polyphony

a cappella

MUSIC & HISTORY

To learn more about the Renaissance period, see page 100.

Focus

- Describe and perform homophony and polyphony.
- Sing music in a madrigal style.
- Perform music representing the Renaissance period.

Getting Started

Do you know any modern-day "Renaissance" men or women? Today we use that term for a person with a wide variety of interests and expertise. English composer Thomas Morley (1557–1602) could be considered an original Renaissance man. Not only did he live during the **Renaissance period** *(c. 1430–1600)*, he was a successful businessman, entrepreneur, organist, composer and teacher. Morley also wrote one of the most important instruction manuals of the time for vocal music and composition, "A Plaine and Easie Introduction to Practicall Musicke"(1597). He must have also been very wise and humble, because in the manual he wrote:

"…never think so well of yourself, but let other men praise you, if you are praiseworthy: then may you justly take it to yourself, so long as it is done with moderation and without arrogance."

That is still good advice for us to remember today.

◆ History and Culture

Thomas Morley is best known as a composer of **madrigals,** or *short secular choral pieces written in the common language, usually with themes of love.* During the Renaissance, **homophony** *(a type of music in which there are two or more parts with similar or identical rhythms being sung or played at the same time)* and **polyphony** *(a type of music in which there are two or more different melodic lines being sung at the same time)* were used in music to create harmony. Examples of both are found in "Now Is The Month Of Maying."

Links to Learning

◆ Theory

The following phrases are examples of homophony and polyphony. Read and perform each phrase using solfège syllables or a neutral syllable.

Homophony

Polyphony

◆ Artistic Expression

The term *madrigal style* now refers to the light, delicate and clearly articulated singing that is necessary for each independent **a cappella** *(singing without instrumental accompaniment)* vocal line to fit together. Work in small groups with other singers on your voice part until you can sing your part cleanly, expressively and as if you were singing a solo line.

Evaluation

Demonstrate how well you have learned the concepts and skills presented in "Now Is The Month Of Maying" by completing the following:

- Define *homophony* and *polyphony*. Locate examples of each in the music. Share your findings with a classmate and decide if your choices were correct.

- In a trio with one singer on a part, sing measures 1–8 to demonstrate "madrigal style" singing. This includes a light, delicate tone and clear articulation. Decide how well you did.

Now Is The Month Of Maying

Arranged by
SHERRI PORTERFIELD

THOMAS MORLEY
(1557–1602)

Der Herr segne euch

Composer: Johann Sebastian Bach (1685–1750), arranged by Barry Talley
Text: Psalm 115:14
Voicing: TB

VOCABULARY

cantata

Baroque period

head voice

chest voice

counterpoint

MUSIC & HISTORY

To learn more about the Baroque period, see page 104.

Focus

- Identify and perform music written in counterpoint.

- Demonstrate musical artistry through the use of proper German diction.

- Describe and perform music from the Baroque period.

Getting Started

Imagine having a piece of music composed specifically for you! This is exactly what happened when German composer Johann Sebastian Bach composed "Der Herr segne euch" as part of a cantata to celebrate a wedding. A **cantata** is *a musical piece made up of several movements for singers and instrumentalists.* "Der Herr segne euch" is a blessing for the wedding couple.

◆ History and Culture

Genius can be defined as "extraordinary intellectual power, especially as manifested in creative activity." German composer Johann Sebastian Bach (1685–1750) was a musical genius. He is considered by many to be the greatest composer who ever lived. In addition to being tremendously gifted, Bach was a diligent student who studied and practiced often.

Bach lived and composed during the **Baroque period** *(1600–1750)*. The music of the Baroque period used harmonic structures differently, through the development of vertical chords. This period also saw the development of new musical forms, such as the cantata. Frequently, the music from this period features a simple melody, supported by a fancy accompaniment with a continuously moving bass line. Bach was such a monumental composer of the Baroque style that the ending date of the Baroque period is actually the year of his death.

Links to Learning

◆ Vocal

Perform the following example to increase ease in singing from your **head voice** *(the higher part of the singer's vocal range)* to your **chest voice** *(the lower part of the singer's vocal range)*. Begin in a light head voice and sing from high to low on "oo" while maintaining good breath support. Repeat the pattern a half step lower each time.

Ooh,_____ ooh,_____ ooh,_____ ooh,_____ ooh,_____ (etc.)

◆ Theory

Counterpoint is *the combination of two or more melodic lines.* The individual melodies constitute the horizontal line while the intervals occurring between them represent the vertical harmony. Bach was a master at composing contrapuntal music. Perform the following example to develop skill in singing two-part counterpoint.

Evaluation

Demonstrate how well you have learned the skills and concepts featured in the lesson "Der Herr segne euch" by completing the following:

• With two to four singers, sing the Theory section above in two parts. Evaluate how well your group was able to sing in two parts written in counterpoint.

• Write the text in German. Beneath the German, write the English translation. Underline the important words in the text. Read the text aloud, stressing the important words in the text. Transfer this word stress to your performance of the piece. Evaluate how well you were able to perform each appropriate word stress.

Der Herr segne euch

(May God Bless You)

For TB and Piano

Arranged by BARRY TALLEY
English translation by J. MARK BAKER

Text from Psalm 115:14
JOHANN SEBASTIAN BACH (1685–1750)

mehr, je mehr und mehr,   je mehr und mehr.
more, for - ev - er - more,   for - ev - er - more.

je mehr und mehr, je mehr und mehr.
for - ev - er - more, for - ev - er - more.

Euch,
You,

Euch,
You,

Ave Verum Corpus

Composer: Wolfgang Amadeus Mozart (1756–1791), arranged by Joyce Eilers
Text: Eucharist hymn
Voicing: TTB

VOCABULARY

Classical period

legato

International Phonetic Alphabet

Focus

- Sing with legato phrasing and proper breath support.
- Sing a Latin text with comprehension and expression.
- Describe and perform music from the Classical period.

Getting Started

A personalized gift from a friend is a joy to receive. People with special talents have the ability to give unique and creative gifts to their family and friends. Match the following people with the gift they might give.

1. Julia Child	**a.** an evening gown
2. Walt Whitman	**b.** a gold bracelet
3. Coco Chanel	**c.** a nature poem
4. Mickey Mantle	**d.** a French dessert
5. Charles Tiffany	**e.** an autographed baseball

And, of course, if you were a friend of Wolfgang Amadeus Mozart, you might receive a song.

MUSIC HISTORY

To learn more about the Classical period, see page 108.

◆ History and Culture

Wolfgang Amadeus Mozart (1756–1791), one of the most famous composers in Western music, lived and worked in Vienna, Austria, during the **Classical period** *(1750–1820)*.

In the 1780s, the picturesque village of Baden, Austria, was a one-day carriage ride from Vienna. Mozart and his wife, Constanza, enjoyed frequent trips to Baden. The small parish church in Baden offered comfort and solace to the Mozart family. In appreciation, Mozart wrote the beautiful "Ave Verum Corpus" as a gift for the church chorus master, Anton Stoll. The compact and simple 46 measure song was probably first performed by Stoll's amateur church choir. It is often described as a masterpiece of calm repose and dignity. What a gift it has proven to be!

Links to Learning

◆ Vocal

The long **legato** (*a style of singing that is connected and sustained*) phrases in "Ave Verum Corpus" give singers the opportunity to develop proper breath support. One technique for good breath support is to breathe slowly and breathe early. As the introduction is played, begin a slow, deep breath at the indicated places and sing the first phrase softly on "doo" in a comfortable octave. Practice singing the entire phrase in one breath.

◆ Artistic Expression

The **International Phonetic Alphabet** (IPA), developed in Paris, France, in 1886, is *a phonetic alphabet that provides a notational standard for all languages.* The following chart shows the IPA symbols for the Latin vowels. Recite the text of "Ave Verum Corpus" using only the following sounds for the vowels.

Written	Pronounced	IPA	Transliterated
a	f<u>a</u>ther	[ɑ]	ah
e	f<u>e</u>d	[ɛ]	eh
i	f<u>ee</u>t	[i]	ee
o	f<u>ou</u>ght	[ɔ]	aw
u	f<u>oo</u>d	[u]	oo

Evaluation

Demonstrate how well you have learned the skills and concepts presented in the lesson "Ave Verum Corpus" by completing the following:

- Find two 4-measure phrases in "Ave Verum Corpus" that you are able to sing in one breath, and perform these phrases for a friend. How did you do?

- With a friend, recite the text of "Ave Verum Corpus," alternately speaking every four measures. Listen to each other and check for correct pronunciation. Decide which words of the text need more practice.

Ave Verum Corpus

For TTB and Piano (may be sung a cappella)

Arranged by
JOYCE EILERS

WOLFGANG AMADEUS MOZART
(1756–1791)

* If performed a cappella, omit bracketed measures
** Tempo is suggested by arranger

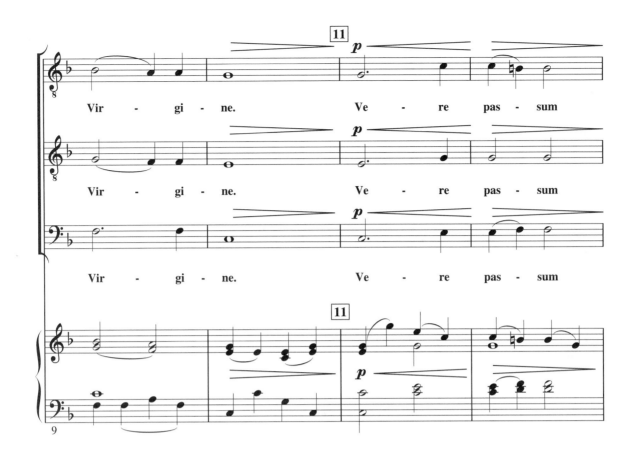

Vir - gi - ne. Ve - re pas - sum

Vir - gi - ne. Ve - re pas - sum

Vir - gi - ne. Ve - re pas - sum

im - mo - la - tum in cru - ce pro

im - mo - la - tum in cru - ce pro

im - mo - la - tum in cru - ce pro

ra - tum un - da flu - xit et san - gui -

ne. Es - to no - bis prae - gus -

ta - tum in mor - tis ex -

ta - tum in mor - tis ex -

prae - gus - ta - tum in mor - tis ex -

a - mi - ne, in mor -

a - mi - ne, in mor -

a - mi - ne, in mor -

Da unten im Tale

Composer: German Folk Song, arranged by Johannes Brahms (1833–1897)
Text: Barry Talley
Voicing: TB

VOCABULARY

lied

Romantic period

unison

interval

third

Focus

- Perform harmony with intervals of a third.
- Read and perform dotted quarter notes.
- Describe and perform music from the Romantic period.

Getting Started

…The joys of love and the sorrows of love…

There are a lot of songs about love—some are happy and some are sad. Whether of joy or sorrow, the songs of love frequently have captivating melodies and poignant words. As for the sad love songs, have you ever heard of these classic break-up songs?

"In My Life" by The Beatles

"Fifty Ways To Leave Your Lover" by Paul Simon

"Don't It Make My Brown Eyes Blue" by Crystal Gayle

"Loving Arms" by The Dixie Chicks

If there were a classic break-up song list from the nineteenth century, "Da unten im Tale" by Johannes Brahms would certainly be on it.

MUSIC & HISTORY

To learn more about the Romantic period,
see page 112.

◆ History and Culture

"Da unten im Tale" ("Below in the Valley") is a German **lied,** or *a song in the German language, generally with a secular text.* It is based on a traditional folk song. Born in Hamburg, Germany, Johannes Brahms (1833–1897) was a prominent composer of the **Romantic period** *(1820–1900).* The lyrical, uncluttered and rich style that Brahms used in his instrumental and choral pieces also enhanced his settings of folk songs. These songs often dealt with the joys and sorrows of love. It is interesting to note that although Brahms was an expert at writing love songs, he remained a bachelor his entire life.

Links to Learning

◆ Vocal

Read and perform the following example in **unison** *(all parts singing the same notes at the same time)* and then as a round. Sing only those pitches that are within your range. When you sing in a round, listen to the **interval** *(the distance between two notes)* formed between the scale pitches. This interval is a **third** *(an interval of two pitches that are three notes apart on the staff)* and is found often in "Da unten im Tale."

◆ Theory

In music notation, the dot next to a note increases the length of that note by half its value. Therefore, a dotted quarter note is one and a half beats long. Read and perform the following rhythmic patterns while keeping a steady tempo. When singing, sustain the dotted quarter notes for their full value.

Evaluation

Demonstrate how well you have learned the skills and concepts presented in "Da unten im Tale" by completing the following:

- In a tenor-bass duet consisting of yourself and one other singer, sing measures 4–8 to show that you can sing harmony with intervals of a third. Discuss how well you did.

- Alone or in a small group, sing measures 4–12 to show the difference in the rhythmic patterns of measures 5–7 and measures 9–10. How well were you able to show a distinction between the two patterns?

- Compose a four-measure melodic phrase in $\frac{3}{4}$ meter. Use some dotted quarter notes and vary your rhythmic patterns. Begin and end your melody on *do,* as seen in the Vocal section above. Share your melodic phrase with a classmate and check for rhythmic and melodic accuracy.

Da unten im Tale

(Down There in the Valley)

For TB and Piano

Choral arrangement by BARRY TALLEY
English translation by J. MARK BAKER

German Folk Song arranged by
JOHANNES BRAHMS (1833–1897)

Music & History

Links to Music

Renaissance Period 100
   Now Is The Month Of Maying 66

Baroque Period 104
   Der Herr segne euch 74

Classical Period 108
   Ave Verum Corpus 86

Romantic Period 112
   Da unten im Tale 94

Contemporary Period 116
   Be Cool 14

Sandro Botticelli (1445–1510) was an Italian painter who lived and worked in Florence, Italy, during the Renaissance. *The Adoration of the Magi* reflects the Renaissance interest in religious subjects. Framing the central figures within the strong geometric pillars emphasized those figures over others. Botticelli was also commissioned by the Pope to paint frescoes in the Sistine Chapel in the Vatican.

Sandro Botticelli. *The Adoration of the Magi.* c. 1480. Tempera and oil on panel. 70.2 x 104.2 cm (27 5/8 x 41"). National Gallery of Art, Washington, D. C. Andrew W. Mellon Collection.

Focus

- Describe the Renaissance period, including important developments.
- Describe characteristics of Renaissance music.

The Renaissance— A Time of Exploration

The **Renaissance period** *(1430–1600)* was a time during the fifteenth and sixteenth centuries of rapid development in exploration, science, art and music. This period could be called the beginning of modern history and the beginning of Western civilization as we know it now.

The development and use of the compass as a navigational aid in China made it possible for explorers to travel to new continents and to discover other cultures. Renaissance sailors first took to the seas to supply Europeans with Asian spices such as peppercorns, nutmeg and cinnamon. Also from the East came precious jewels and fine silk, a fabric especially valued for women's clothing.

Sailors also brought back information and customs from other cultures. This new information, along with a revived interest in writings from the ancient Greek and Roman cultures, was quickly spread across Europe, thanks to the invention of the printing press and mass-produced books. The invention of the printing press, credited to Johann Gutenberg, was one of the most significant developments of the Renaissance. As books became more available and less expensive, more people learned to read and began to consider new ideas.

A major change in the Christian religion occurred at this time. During the Protestant Reformation, various groups of Christians left the Catholic Church and formed some of the present-day Protestant denominations. Many Protestant groups translated Bibles from the Catholic Church's language of Latin to the language spoken by the people.

Remarkable advances were made in the arts and sciences by:

- Thomas Weelkes—English composer
- Gerardus Mercator—German mapmaker
- Vasco da Gama—Portuguese explorer who rounded the Horn of Africa and went on to India

COMPOSERS

Josquin des Prez
(c. 1450–1521)

Andrea Gabrieli
(c. 1510–1586)

Michael Praetorius
(1571–1621)

Thomas Weelkes
(c. 1576–1623)

ARTISTS

Gentile Bellini
(1429–1507)

Sandro Botticelli
(1445–1510)

Leonardo da Vinci
(1452–1519)

Michelangelo
(1475–1564)

Raphael
(1483–1520)

AUTHORS

Martin Luther
(1483–1546)

William Shakespeare
(1565–1616)

VOCABULARY

Renaissance period

sacred music

mass

motet

secular music

lute

polyphony

a cappella

madrigal

word painting

Renaissance Music

During the Renaissance, the Catholic Church gradually lost some of its influence over the daily lives of people. Much of the important music of the period, however, was still **sacred music**, or *music associated with religious services and themes*. In music, a **mass** is *a religious service of prayers and ceremonies*. A **motet** is *a shorter choral work, also set to a Latin text and used in religious services, but not part of the regular mass*. These two types of compositions were the most important forms of sacred Renaissance music. In Protestant churches, sacred music was composed and sung in the languages of the worshippers.

Like sacred music, **secular music**, or *music not associated with religious services or themes*, flourished during the Renaissance period. The center of musical activity gradually began to shift from churches to castles and towns. Music became an important form of entertainment for members of the emerging middle class. Social dancing became more widespread. Dance music of this period was written for **lute**, *an early form of the guitar*, and other instruments.

The Renaissance period is often referred to as the "golden age of polyphony." **Polyphony**, which literally means "many-sounding," is *a type of music in which there are two or more different melodic lines being sung or played at the same time*. Much of the choral music of the time was polyphonic, with as many as sixteen different vocal parts. Instruments were sometimes used to accompany and echo the voices.

Performance Links

When performing music of the Renaissance period, it is important to apply the following guidelines:

- Sing with clarity and purity of tone.
- Balance the vocal lines with equal importance.
- In polyphonic music, sing the rhythms accurately and with precision.
- When designated by the composer, sing **a cappella** (*unaccompanied or without instruments*).

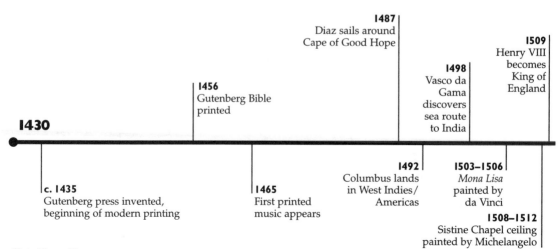

1487
Diaz sails around
Cape of Good Hope

1509
Henry VIII
becomes
King of
England

1498
Vasco da
Gama
discovers
sea route
to India

1456
Gutenberg Bible
printed

1430

c. 1435
Gutenberg press invented,
beginning of modern printing

1465
First printed
music appears

1492
Columbus lands
in West Indies/
Americas

1503–1506
Mona Lisa
painted by
da Vinci

1508–1512
Sistine Chapel ceiling
painted by Michelangelo

Listening Links

CHORAL SELECTION
"As Vesta Was Descending" by Thomas Weelkes (c.1576–1623)

Thomas Weelkes was an important English composer and organist. "As Vesta Was Descending" is an outstanding example of a **madrigal**, *a musical setting of a poem in three or more parts*. Generally, a madrigal has a secular text and is sung a cappella. This madrigal was written in honor of Queen Elizabeth I of England. This piece is an excellent example of **word painting**, *a technique in which the music reflects the meaning of the words*. Listen carefully to discover what occurs in the music on the following words: "descending," "ascending," "running down amain," "two by two," "three by three," and "all alone." Why do you think Weelkes chose to use the repeated text at the end?

INSTRUMENTAL SELECTION
"Three Voltas" from *Terpsichore* by Michael Praetorius (1571–1621)

During the Renaissance, a favorite type of composition involved a combination of dances in changing tempos and meters. Some of the dance music developed into stylized pieces for listening, which were not intended for actual dancing. *Terpsichore*, by German composer Michael Praetorius, is a collection of 312 short dance pieces, written in four, five or six parts, with no particular instrumentation specified.

You will hear authentic early instruments in this recording. By listening carefully, guess which modern-day instruments are descended from these early ones.

Check Your Understanding

1. List three major nonmusical changes that took place during the Renaissance period.
2. Describe polyphony as heard in "As Vesta Was Descending."
3. Describe how music from the Renaissance is different from music of today.

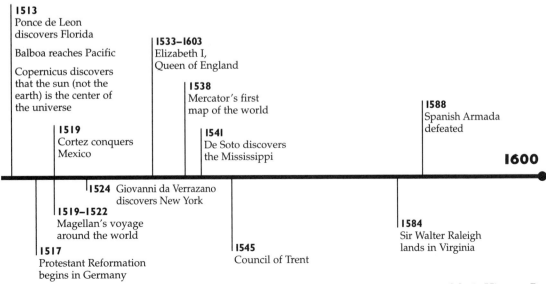

1513
Ponce de Leon
discovers Florida

Balboa reaches Pacific

Copernicus discovers
that the sun (not the
earth) is the center of
the universe

1519
Cortez conquers
Mexico

1533–1603
Elizabeth I,
Queen of England

1538
Mercator's first
map of the world

1541
De Soto discovers
the Mississippi

1588
Spanish Armada
defeated

1600

1524 Giovanni da Verrazano
discovers New York

1519–1522
Magellan's voyage
around the world

1517
Protestant Reformation
begins in Germany

1545
Council of Trent

1584
Sir Walter Raleigh
lands in Virginia

 The work of the Italian painter Orazio Gentileschi (1563–1639) was influenced by the innovative style of Caravaggio. In later years, Orazio's works tend to place a single figure or a restricted figure group in sharp relief before a dark background. The subject of this painting, St. Cecilia, is often referred to as the patron saint of music. She is playing a small table pipe organ.

Orazio Gentileschi. *Saint Cecilia and an Angel*. c. 1610. Oil on canvas. 87.8 x 108.1 cm (34 5/8 x 42 1/2"). National Gallery of Art, Washington, D. C. Samuel H. Kress Collection.

Focus

- Describe the Baroque period, including important developments.
- Describe characteristics of Baroque music.

The Baroque Period— A Time of Elaboration

The **Baroque period** *(1600–1750)* was a time of powerful kings and their courts. In Europe, elaborate clothing, hats and hairstyles for the wealthy men and women matched the decorated buildings, gardens, furniture and paintings of this period. The term *baroque* comes from a French word for "imperfect or irregular pearls." Often, pearls were used as decorations on clothing.

There was a great interest in science and exploration. During the Baroque period, Galileo perfected the telescope by 1610, providing the means for greater exploration of the universe. Sir Isaac Newton identified gravity and formulated principles of physics and mathematics. Bartolomeo Cristofori developed the modern pianoforte in which hammers strike the strings. Exploration of new worlds continued, and colonization of places discovered during the Renaissance increased.

Most paintings and sculptures of the time were characterized by their large scale and dramatic details. Artwork celebrated the splendor of royal rulers. For example, the Palace at Versailles near Paris, was built and decorated as a magnificent setting for King Louis XIV of France. It features notably elaborate architecture, paintings, sculptures and gardens.

The Baroque period was a time of great changes brought about through the work of extraordinary people such as:

- Johann Sebastian Bach—German composer
- Orazio Gentileschi—Italian painter
- Alexander Pope—English poet
- Galileo Galilei—Italian mathematician who used his new telescope to prove that the Milky Way is made up of individual stars

COMPOSERS

Johann Pachelbel
(1653–1706)

Antonio Vivaldi
(1678–1741)

Johann Sebastian Bach
(1685–1750)

George Frideric Handel
(1685–1759)

ARTISTS

El Greco
(1541–1614)

Orazio Gentileschi
(1563–1639)

Peter Paul Rubens
(1577–1640)

Rembrandt van Rijn
(1606–1669)

Jan Steen
(1626–1679)

Jan Vermeer
(1632–1675)

AUTHORS

Ben Jonson
(1572–1637)

René Descartes
(1596–1650)

John Milton
(1608–1674)

Molière
(1622–1673)

Alexander Pope
(1688–1744)

Samuel Johnson
(1709–1784)

VOCABULARY

Baroque period

basso continuo

opera

oratorio

concerto grosso

Baroque Music

The music of the Baroque period shows the same kind of dramatic flair that characterized the clothing, architecture and art of the time. Most of the compositions of that period have a strong sense of movement, often including a **basso continuo**, or *a continually moving bass line*.

The Baroque period brought about a great interest in instrumental music. Keyboard instruments were refined, including the clavichord, harpsichord and organ. The modern string family of instruments were now used, and the trumpet became a favorite melody instrument in orchestras.

During the Baroque period, a number of new forms of music were developed. **Opera**, *a combination of singing, instrumental music, dancing and drama that tells a story*, was created beginning with *Orfeo*, by Claudio Monteverdi (1567–1643). The **oratorio**, *a large-scale work for solo voices, chorus and orchestra based on a literary or religious theme*, was also developed. In 1741, George Frideric Handel (1685–1759) composed the *Messiah*, one of the most famous oratorios still performed today. The **concerto grosso** (*a multi-movement Baroque piece for a group of soloists and an orchestra*) was also made popular with Antonio Vivaldi's (1678–1741) *The Four Seasons* and Johann Sebastian Bach's (1685–1750) *Brandenberg Concertos*.

Performance Links

When performing music of the Baroque period, it is important to apply the following guidelines:

- Sing with accurate pitch.
- Be conscious of who has the dominant theme and make sure the accompanying part or parts do not overshadow the melody.
- Keep a steady, unrelenting pulse in most pieces. Precision of dotted rhythms is especially important.
- When dynamic level changes occur, all vocal lines need to change together.

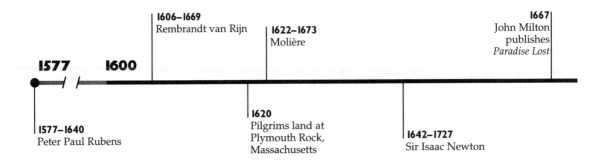

Listening Links

CHORAL SELECTION

"Gloria in excelsis Deo" from *Gloria in D Major* by Antonio Vivaldi (1678–1741)

Antonio Vivaldi was one of the greatest composers and violinists of his time. He wrote operas and concertos, as well as sacred works (oratorios, motets and masses) for chorus, soloists and orchestra. One of his most popular choral works is the *Gloria in D Major* mass. "Gloria in excelsis Deo" is a magnificent choral piece. It is full of energy and emotion that is expressed with great drama. It was composed for three solo voices and chorus, and is accompanied by a variety of instruments. Does ornamentation occur in the vocal parts, in the accompaniment, or both?

INSTRUMENTAL SELECTION

"The Arrival of the Queen of Sheba" from *Solomon* by George Frideric Handel (1685–1759)

George Frideric Handel was a German-born composer who lived in England for most of his life. The oratorio *Solomon* tells the story of King Solomon, of tenth-century Israel. Solomon was known for his great wisdom. Sheba, the Queen of Ethiopia, came to visit and challenge Solomon, but he wisely answered all her questions, and she left as an ally. *Solomon* was written for two choruses, five soloists, a chamber orchestra and a harpsichord. Two instruments are featured playing a duet in this piece. What is the name of these instruments, and to what instrument family do they belong?

Check Your Understanding

1. List three major nonmusical developments that took place during the Baroque period.

2. How would the performance of the oratorio *Solomon* differ from the performance of an opera?

3. Describe how music from the Baroque period is different from music of the Renaissance.

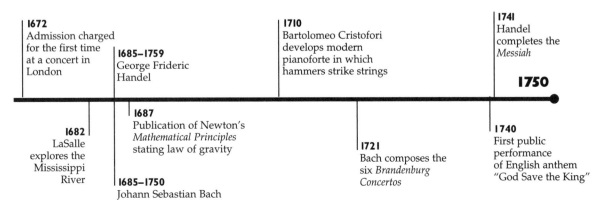

| 1672 Admission charged for the first time at a concert in London | 1685–1759 George Frideric Handel | | 1710 Bartolomeo Cristofori develops modern pianoforte in which hammers strike strings | | 1741 Handel completes the *Messiah* |

1682 LaSalle explores the Mississippi River

1687 Publication of Newton's *Mathematical Principles* stating law of gravity

1685–1750 Johann Sebastian Bach

1721 Bach composes the six *Brandenburg Concertos*

1750

1740 First public performance of English anthem "God Save the King"

French artist Elisabeth Vigée-LeBrun (1755–1842) lived and worked in Paris during the time of the French Revolution and was forced to flee the city in disguise in 1789. A majority of Vigeé-LeBrun paintings are portraits of women and children. This painting expresses friendship and maternal love.

Elisabeth Vigée-LeBrun. *The Marquise de Pezé and the Marquise de Rouget with Her Two Children.* 1787. Oil on canvas. 123.4 x 155.9 cm (48 5/8 x 61 3/8"). National Gallery of Art, Washington, D. C. Gift of the Bay Foundation in memory of Josephine Bay and Ambassador Charles Ulrick Bay.

Focus

- Describe the Classical period, including important developments.
- Describe characteristics of Classical music.

The Classical Period— A Time of Balance, Clarity and Simplicity

The **Classical period** *(1750–1820)* was a time when people became influenced by the early Greeks and Romans for examples of order and ways of living life. Travelers of the period visited the ruins of ancient Egypt, Rome and Greece and brought the ideas of the ancients to the art and architecture of the time. As a result, the calm beauty and simplicity of this classical art from the past inspired artists and musicians to move away from the overly decorated styles of the Baroque period. The music, art and architecture reflected a new emphasis on emotional restraint and simplicity.

In the intellectual world, there was increasing emphasis on individual reason and enlightenment. Writers such as Voltaire and Thomas Jefferson suggested that through science and democracy, rather than mystery and monarchy, people could choose their own fate. Such thinking, brought on by the enlarging middle class and the excesses of the wealthy royal class, was the beginning of important political changes in society. In many parts of Europe, the power and authority of royalty were attacked, and members of the middle class struggled for their rights. There was a revolution against England by the American colonies, which resulted in the establishment of the United States. In France, the monarchy was overthrown, and the king and most of his court were beheaded.

Some of the most important contributors of the time were:

- Wolfgang Amadeus Mozart—Austrian composer
- Elisabeth Vigée-Lebrun—French painter
- Ben Franklin—American writer, inventor, diplomat
- Joseph Priestley—English chemist who discovered oxygen
- Robert Fulton—American inventor who produced the

COMPOSERS

Carl Philipp Emanuel Bach
(1714–1788)

Johann Christian Bach
(1735–1762)

Franz Joseph Haydn
(1732–1809)

Wolfgang Amadeus Mozart
(1756–1791)

Ludwig van Beethoven
(1770–1827)

ARTISTS

Louis de Carmontelle
(1717–1806)

Thomas Gainsborough
(1727–1788)

Francisco Göya
(1746–1828)

Jacques-Louis David
(1748–1825)

Elisabeth Vigée-Lebrun
(1755–1842)

AUTHORS

Voltaire
(1694–1778)

Benjamin Franklin
(1706–1790)

William Wordsworth
(1770–1850)

Jane Austen
(1775–1817)

VOCABULARY

Classical period

chamber music

symphony

crescendo

decrescendo

sonata-allegro form

Music of the Classical Period

The music of the Classical period was based on balance, clarity and simplicity. Like the architecture of ancient Greece, music was fit together in "building blocks" by balancing one four-bar phrase against another. Classical music was more restrained than the music of the Baroque period, when flamboyant embellishments were common.

The piano replaced the harpsichord and became a favorite instrument of composers. Many concertos were written for the piano. The string quartet was a popular form of **chamber music** *(music performed by a small instrumental ensemble, generally with one instrument per part)*. The **symphony** *(a large-scale work for orchestra)* was also a common type of music during this period. Orchestras continued to develop and expand into four families: brass, percussion, strings and woodwinds. Other forms, such as the opera, mass and oratorio, continued to develop as well.

Two major composers associated with the Classical period are Franz Joseph Haydn (1732–1809) and Wolfgang Amadeus Mozart (1756–1791). A third major composer, Ludwig van Beethoven (1770–1827), began composing during this period. Beethoven's works bridge the gap between the Classical and Romantic periods, and are discussed in the next period.

Performance Links

When performing music of the Classical period, it is important to apply the following guidelines:

- Listen for the melody line so the accompaniment parts do not overshadow it.
- Sing chords in tune.
- Make dynamic level changes that move smoothly through each **crescendo** *(a dynamic marking that indicates to gradually sing or play louder)* and **decrescendo** *(a dynamic marking that indicates to gradually sing or play softer)*.
- Keep phrases flowing and connected.

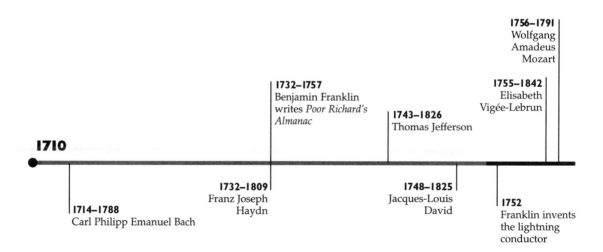

Listening Links

CHORAL SELECTION

"The Heavens Are Telling" from *Creation* by Franz Joseph Haydn (1732–1809)

Franz Joseph Haydn was an Austrian composer who was Beethoven's teacher, and Mozart's friend. The *Creation* is an oratorio based on a poem from John Milton's *Paradise Lost* and the first chapters of the book of Genesis from the Bible. The angels Gabriel, Uriel and Raphael are portrayed by three soloists, and they describe events of each day of the creation. "The Heavens Are Telling" is a grand celebration of praise that alternates between the full chorus and the trio of soloists. List the order of the choral voice parts in the imitative section as they enter with the words, "With wonders of His work."

INSTRUMENTAL SELECTION

Eine Kleine Nachtmusik, First Movement by Wolfgang Amadeus Mozart (1756–1791)

Wolfgang Amadeus Mozart, another Austrian composer, began his musical career at an extremely early age. By the time he was four years old, Mozart had already mastered the keyboard, and by age five, he had written his first composition. Considered one of the greatest composers of all time, he composed 600 musical works.

The first movement of *Eine Kleine Nachtmusik* is written in **sonata-allegro form**, *a large ABA form consisting of three sections: exposition, development and recapitulation.* The Exposition (section A) presents two themes: (a) and (b). Next comes the Development section (section B). The Recapitulation is a return to the original theme (a). Listen to this selection and write down the name for each section of the sonata-allegro form as you hear it.

Check Your Understanding

1. List three major nonmusical changes that took place during the Classical period.

2. Describe the characteristics of Classical music heard in *Eine Kleine Nachtmusik*.

3. Describe how music from the Classical period is different from music of the Baroque period.

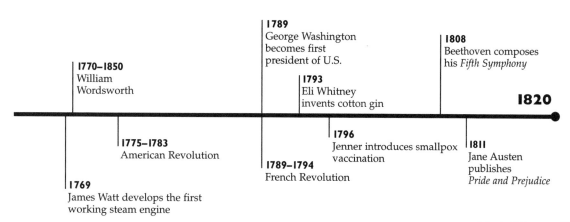

1789
George Washington becomes first president of U.S.

1808
Beethoven composes his *Fifth Symphony*

1770–1850
William Wordsworth

1793
Eli Whitney invents cotton gin

1820

1775–1783
American Revolution

1796
Jenner introduces smallpox vaccination

1811
Jane Austen publishes *Pride and Prejudice*

1789–1794
French Revolution

1769
James Watt develops the first working steam engine

The American artist George Caleb Bingham (1811–1879) was born in Virginia and raised in Missouri. He became known for his river scenes, often of boatmen bringing cargo to the American West along the Missouri and Mississippi rivers. The scene here is a group of boatmen on a flatboat amusing themselves with their own music and dancing.

George Caleb Bingham. *The Jolly Flatboatmen*. 1846. Oil on canvas. 96.9 x 123.2 cm (38 1/8 x 48 1/2"). National Gallery of Art, Washington, D. C. Private Collection.

Focus

- Describe the Romantic period, including important developments.
- Describe characteristics of Romantic music.

The Romantic Period— A Time of Drama

A new sense of political and artistic freedom emerged during the **Romantic period** *(1820–1900)*. The period began in the middle of the Industrial Revolution, a time when manufacturing became mechanized and many people left farm life to work and live in cities where the manufacturing plants were located. Scientific and mechanical achievements were made in the development of railroads, steamboats, the telegraph and telephone, photography, and sound recordings.

The Industrial Revolution caused a major change in the economic and social life of the common people and also produced a wealthy middle class. More people were able to take part in cultural activities, such as attending music performances and going to art museums. Musicians and artists experienced greater freedom to express their individual creative ideas. This was because they were able to support themselves by ticket sales or sales of their art, instead of relying on the patronage of royalty or the church.

As people moved into the cities, nature and life in the country became the inspiration for many artists. The paintings of William Turner expressed the feelings suggested by nature. Later, French Impressionistic painters, including Claude Monet and Pierre-Auguste Renoir, developed new techniques bringing nature and natural light alive for the viewer.

Some of the most prominent thinkers and creators of this period were:

- Georges Bizet—French composer
- George Caleb Bingham—American painter
- Charles Dickens—English author
- Samuel F. B. Morse—American inventor who developed the telegraph

COMPOSERS

Ludwig van Beethoven (1770–1827)

Franz Schubert (1797–1828)

Felix Mendelssohn (1809–1847)

Frédéric Chopin (1810–1849)

Franz Liszt (1811–1886)

Richard Wagner (1813–1883)

Giuseppe Verdi (1813–1901)

Bedrich Smetana (1824–1884)

Johannes Brahms (1833–1897)

Georges Bizet (1838–1875)

Peter Ilyich Tchaikovsky (1840–1893)

Antonín Dvořák (1841–1904)

Claude Debussy (1862–1918)

ARTISTS

George Caleb Bingham (1811–1879)

Edgar Degas (1834–1917)

Paul Cezanne (1839–1906)

Auguste Rodin (1840–1917)

Claude Monet (1840–1926)

Pierre-Auguste Renoir (1841–1919)

Mary Cassatt (1845–1926)

Paul Gauguin (1848–1903)

Vincent van Gogh (1853–1890)

AUTHORS

Alexandre Dumas (1802–1870)

Henry Wadsworth Longfellow (1807–1882)

Charles Dickens (1812–1870)

Jules Verne (1828–1905)

Louisa May Alcott (1832–1884)

Mark Twain (1835–1910)

Rudyard Kipling (1865–1905)

VOCABULARY

Romantic period

music critic

overture

symphonic poem

Music of the Romantic Period

Music of the Romantic period focused on both the heights and depths of human emotion. The new musical ideas were expressed through larger works with complex vocal melodies and colorful harmonies. During this time, most of the brass and woodwind instruments developed into what they are today, and these instruments were used to add more tone and depth to the music.

Composers began to think about selling their music to the new audiences of middle-class people. Two types of music that appealed to these audiences were the extravagant spectacles of opera and the boldness of grand symphonic music. As music became public, it became subject to public scrutiny, particularly by music critics. A **music critic** is *a writer who gives an evaluation of a musical performance.*

Much of the music of the time was related to literature, such as Felix Mendelssohn's (1809–1847) *A Midsummer Night's Dream*, which was based on the play by William Shakespeare. A well-known section of this work is the **overture**, or *a piece for orchestra that serves as an introduction to an opera or other dramatic work.* The **symphonic poem** is *a single-movement work for orchestra, inspired by a painting, play or other literary or visual work.* Franz Liszt (1811–1886) was a prominent composer of this style of music. The Romantic period was also a time of nationalism, which was reflected in works such as Liszt's *Hungarian Dances*, Richard Wagner's focus on Germanic music, and the tributes to Italy found in Giuseppe Verdi's operas.

Performance Links

When performing music of the Romantic period, it is important to apply the following guidelines:

- Understand the relation of the text to the melody and harmony.
- Concentrate on phrasing, and maintain a clear, beautiful melodic line.
- Perform accurately the wide range of dynamics and tempos.
- Sing confidently in foreign languages to reflect nationalism in music.

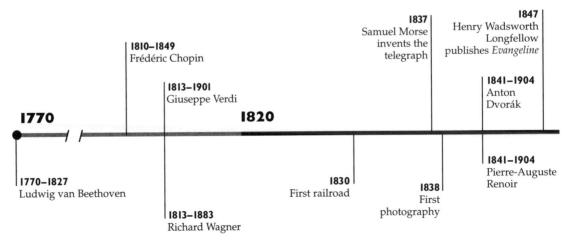

1810–1849 Frédéric Chopin

1813–1901 Giuseppe Verdi

1837 Samuel Morse invents the telegraph

1847 Henry Wadsworth Longfellow publishes *Evangeline*

1841–1904 Anton Dvorák

1770

1820

1770–1827 Ludwig van Beethoven

1813–1883 Richard Wagner

1830 First railroad

1838 First photography

1841–1904 Pierre-Auguste Renoir

Listening Links

CHORAL SELECTION
"Toreador Chorus" from *Carmen* by Georges Bizet (1838–1875)

Carmen, by French composer Georges Bizet, is considered to be one of the most popular operas ever written. The opera tells the story of a gypsy girl who is arrested when she gets into a fight. Placed in the custody of the soldier Don Jose, Carmen soon entices him into a love affair. She then meets Escamilio, a toreador (bullfighter), and tries to get rid of Don Jose. Jilted, Don Jose stabs Carmen and kills himself. The "Toreador Chorus" is heard during the Procession of the Bullfighters. As you listen to the music, write two or three sentences to describe this procession scene in the opera as you think it would look.

INSTRUMENTAL SELECTION
"The Moldau" by Bedrich Smetana (1824–1884)

Bedrich Smetana was a prominent Czech composer. Smetana had a passion for music and composed in spite of his father's desire for him to become a lawyer. His musical efforts were focused mainly on trying to produce Czech national music based on the folk songs and dances that already existed. Smetana awoke one morning to find himself totally deaf. This created a depression that stayed with him through the remainder of his life. "The Moldau" represents Smetana's deep feeling about the beauty and significance of the river that flows through the city of Prague.

Check Your Understanding

1. List three major nonmusical changes that took place during the Romantic period.

2. Describe how "The Moldau" reflects nationalism in music of the Romantic period.

3. Describe how music of the Romantic period is different from music of another period.

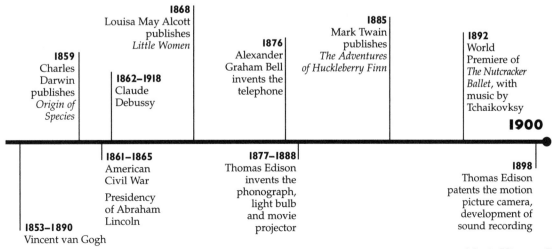

1859
Charles
Darwin
publishes
*Origin of
Species*

1868
Louisa May Alcott
publishes
Little Women

1862–1918
Claude
Debussy

1876
Alexander
Graham Bell
invents the
telephone

1885
Mark Twain
publishes
*The Adventures
of Huckleberry Finn*

1892
World
Premiere of
*The Nutcracker
Ballet*, with
music by
Tchaikovksy

1900

1853–1890
Vincent van Gogh

1861–1865
American
Civil War

Presidency
of Abraham
Lincoln

1877–1888
Thomas Edison
invents the
phonograph,
light bulb
and movie
projector

1898
Thomas Edison
patents the motion
picture camera,
development of
sound recording

African American artist Romare Howard Bearden (1911–1988) is recognized as one of the most creative visual artists of the twentieth century. He experimented with many different styles and mediums but found a unique form of expression in collage. He had a great interest in literature, history, music, mathematics and the performing arts.

Romare Bearden. *The Piano Lesson (Homage to Mary Lou)*. 1983. Color lithograph on paper. 75.2 x 52.3 cm (29 1/2 x 20 1/2"). The Pennsylvania Academy of the Fine Arts, Philadelphia, Pennsylvania. The Harold A. and Ann R. Sorgenti Collection of Contemporary African American Art.

Focus

- Describe the Contemporary period, including important developments.
- Describe characteristics of Contemporary music.

The Contemporary Period— The Search for Originality

Nothing characterizes the **Contemporary period** *(1900–present)* better than technology. Many technological advances began on October 4, 1957, when the Soviet Union successfully launched *Sputnik I*, the world's first artificial satellite. While the Sputnik launch was a single event, it marked the start of the Space Age and began many new political, military, technological and scientific developments.

Isolation was greatly reduced worldwide by developments in travel (rail, sea and air) and communication (telephone, radio, television and the Internet). It was also reduced as countries came together during World War I and World War II. Elements of cultures merged as people moved from their countries to various parts of the world for economic, political or social reasons. It no longer seems strange, for example, to see Chinese or Mexican restaurants in most communities in the United States or McDonald's® restaurants in Europe and Asia.

Some of the noteworthy leaders of this period have been:

- Igor Stravinsky—Russian/American composer
- Romare Bearden—American artist
- Robert Frost—American poet
- Wilbur and Orville Wright—American inventors who designed and flew the first airplane
- Albert Einstein—German/American scientist who formulated theories of relativity

COMPOSERS

Sergei Rachmaninoff (1873–1943)

Arnold Schoenberg (1874–1951)

Béla Bartók (1881–1945)

Igor Stravinsky (1882–1971)

Sergey Prokofiev (1891–1953)

Carl Orff (1895–1982)

Aaron Copland (1900–1990)

Benjamin Britten (1913–1976)

Leonard Bernstein (1918–1990)

Moses Hogan (1957–2003)

ARTISTS

Henri Matisse (1869–1954)

Pablo Picasso (1881–1973)

Wassily Kandinsky (1866–1944)

Marc Chagall (1887–1985)

Georgia O'Keeffe (1887–1986)

Romare Howard Bearden (1911–1988)

Andy Warhol (1930–1987)

AUTHORS

Robert Frost (1874–1963)

Virginia Woolf (1882–1941)

Ernest Hemingway (1899–1961)

Rachel Carson (1907–1964)

James Baldwin (1924–1997)

JK Rowling (b. 1965)

VOCABULARY

Contemporary period

synthesizer

twelve-tone music

aleatory music

fusion

Music of the Contemporary Period

Technology has had a large influence on Contemporary music. Most people have access to music via radio, television and recordings. Technology has also influenced the music itself. The invention of electrified and electronic instruments led many composers to experiment with the new sounds. One of the most important new instruments was the **synthesizer,** *a musical instrument that produces sounds electronically, rather than by the physical vibrations of an acoustic instrument.*

The Contemporary period has witnessed a number of musical styles. Maurice Ravel (1875–1937) and Claude Debussy (1862–1918), for example, wrote music in the Impressionist style, often describing an impression of nature. Some of the music of Igor Stravinsky (1882–1971) and others was written in a neo-Classical (or "new" classical) style. Other music was considered avant-garde (or unorthodox or experimental); this included Arnold Schoenberg's (1874–1951) **twelve-tone music,** *a type of music that uses all twelve tones of the scale equally.* Composers experimented with **aleatory music,** or *a type of music in which certain aspects are performed randomly and left to chance.*

In addition, composers began using the rhythms, melodies and texts of other cultures in their compositions in a trend called **fusion,** or *the act of combining various types and cultural influences of music into a new style.*

Performance Links

When performing music of the Contemporary period, it is important to apply the following guidelines:

- Sing on pitch, even in extreme parts of your range.
- Tune intervals carefully in the skips found in many melodic lines.
- Sing changing meters and unusual rhythm patterns precisely.
- Perform accurately the wide range of dynamics and tempos.

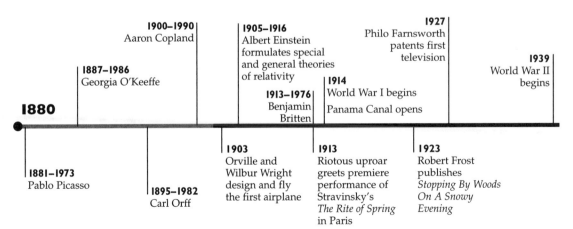

Listening Links

CHORAL SELECTION

"The Battle of Jericho," Traditional Spiritual, arranged by Moses George Hogan (1957–2003)

Moses Hogan, born in New Orleans, Louisiana, was a pianist, conductor and arranger. He has been one of the most influential arrangers of our time in the revitalization of the songs of our forebearers. His contemporary settings of African American spirituals have been revered by audiences and praised by critics. He had a unique talent for expanding the harmonies and rhythms while preserving the traditional essence of these spirituals. Hogan's arrangements have become staples in the repertoires of choirs worldwide. What specific musical effects did Hogan add in his arrangement of "The Battle of Jericho"?

INSTRUMENTAL SELECTION

"Infernal Dance of King Kaschei" from *The Firebird* by Igor Stravinsky (1882–1971)

Igor Stravinsky was born in Russia, but lived the last twenty-five years of his life in California. *The Firebird* is a ballet that begins when Prince Ivan gives a magical golden bird with wings of fire its freedom in return for a feather. With the help of the magic feather, Ivan conquers an evil king and frees the princesses and prisoners that the king had held captive. Prince Ivan falls in love with a princess and they live happily ever after.

In the first section of this piece, you can hear the loud shrieks of the firebird. How many times did you hear this sudden loud sound?

Check Your Understanding

1. List three major nonmusical changes that took place during the Contemporary period.

2. Discuss the differences between a composer and an arranger.

3. Describe how music of the Contemporary period is different from music of the Romantic period.

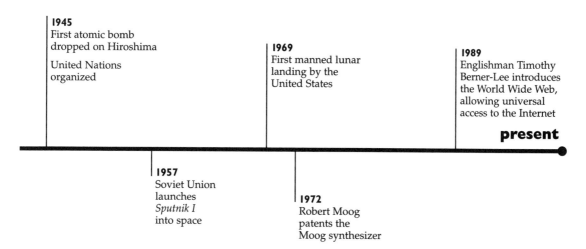

1945
First atomic bomb dropped on Hiroshima

United Nations organized

1957
Soviet Union launches *Sputnik I* into space

1969
First manned lunar landing by the United States

1972
Robert Moog patents the Moog synthesizer

1989
Englishman Timothy Berner-Lee introduces the World Wide Web, allowing universal access to the Internet

present

SPOTLIGHT

Diction

Singing is a form of communication. To communicate well while singing, you must not only form your vowels correctly, but also say your consonants as clearly and cleanly as possible.

There are two kinds of consonants: voiced and unvoiced. Consonants that require the use of the voice along with the **articulators** *(lips, teeth, tongue, and other parts of the mouth and throat)* are called voiced consonants. If you place your hand on your throat, you can actually feel your voice box vibrate while producing them. Unvoiced consonant sounds are made with the articulators only.

In each pair below, the first word contains a voiced consonant while the second word contains an unvoiced consonant. Speak the following word pairs, then sing them on any pitch. When singing, make sure the voiced consonant is on the same pitch as the vowel.

Voiced:	Unvoiced Consonants:	More Voiced Consonants:
[b] bay	[p] pay	[l] lip
[d] den	[t] ten	[m] mice
[g] goat	[k] coat	[n] nice
[ʤ] jeer	[ʧ] cheer	[j] yell
[z] zero	[s] scenic	[r] red
[ʒ] fusion	[ʃ] shun	
[ð] there	[θ] therapy	More Unvoiced Consonants:
[v] vine	[f] fine	[h] have
[w] wince	[hw] whim	

The American "r" requires special treatment in classical choral singing. To sing an American "r" at the end of a syllable following a vowel, sing the vowel with your teeth apart and jaw open. In some formal sacred music and English texts, you may need to flip or roll the "r." For most other instances, sing the "r" on pitch, then open to the following vowel quickly.

Choral Library

The Battle Cry Of Freedom **122**

Come Travel With Me **128**

Frog Went A-Courtin' **140**

Guantanamera **152**

Joshua (Fit the Battle of Jericho) **158**

Leave Her, Johnny **170**

New River Train **174**

On The Deep, Blue Sea **184**

Pretty Saro **198**

Santa Lucia **206**

Sing To The Lord **212**

You Gentlemen Of England **218**

The Battle Cry Of Freedom

Composer: George Frederick Root (1825–1895), arranged by Patti DeWitt
Text: George Frederick Root
Voicing: TB

VOCABULARY

step-wise motion

skip-wise motion

fermata

Focus

- Identify and perform melodies with step-wise and skip-wise motion.
- Read and perform dotted eighth and sixteenth note rhythmic patterns.
- Sing music representing American heritage.

Getting Started

Military historians know that certain songs are associated with particular wars. Sing any of these war favorites that you know.

a. "Yankee Doodle" — from the American Revolutionary War

b. "Over There" — from World War I

c. "God Bless America" — from World War II

d. "Blowin' In The Wind" — from the Vietnam War

e. "From A Distance" — from the 1990 Persian Gulf War

After you learn "The Battle Cry Of Freedom," you can add it to your list as a favorite song from the American Civil War.

 SKILL BUILDERS

To learn more about dotted rhythms, see Intermediate Sight-Singing, *page 89.*

◆ History and Culture

American composer George Frederick Root (1825–1895) wrote sacred and patriotic songs. "The Battle Cry Of Freedom" is the most famous of his 28 Civil War songs. Written after Root had read President Lincoln's proclamation calling for troops, the song was published in 1862. It became a favorite with the civilian population as well as the troops. "The Battle Cry Of Freedom" was played at Fort Sumter on April 14, 1865, when Brigadier General Robert Anderson raised the Union flag over the recaptured fort. The song remained popular with Union as well as Confederate troops.

Links to Learning

◆ Vocal

When Root wrote "The Battle Cry Of Freedom," he used a melody that has **step-wise motion** (*melodic movement from a given note to another note that is directly above or below it on the staff*) and **skip-wise motion** (*melodic movement from a given note to another note that is two or more notes above or below it on the staff*). In a comfortable octave, perform the following example to practice singing step-wise and skip-wise motion. Which do you think is easier to sing?

Yes, we'll   ral - ly 'round   the flag,   boys, we'll   ral - ly once a - gain.

Shout - ing   the bat - tle   cry   of   free - dom.

◆ Theory

Read and perform the following example to practice rhythmic patterns that contain dotted rhythms. Observe the fermata sign over the last note. A **fermata** (⌒) is *a symbol that indicates to hold a note longer than its given value.*

ti ti ta   ti ti ta   tim ka ta   tim ka ta   ta tim ka ti ti ti ti   ta–a   ta

Evaluation

Demonstrate how well you have learned the skills and concepts featured in the lesson "The Battle Cry Of Freedom" by completing the following:

- Locate in the music two examples of melodic step-wise motion and two examples of skip-wise motion. Support your answers by explaining why you made the choices you did.

- Record yourself singing measures 12–22. Play it back and indicate in your music or on a sheet of paper any rhythmic or melodic mistakes. Evaluate how well you were able to perform dotted rhythms correctly.

The Battle Cry Of Freedom

For TB a cappella

Arranged by
PATTI DeWITT

GEORGE FREDERICK ROOT
(1825–1895)

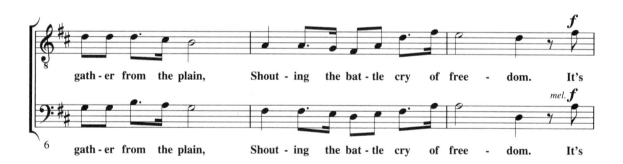

up with the star. While we ral - ly 'round the flag, boys, We'll

up with the star. While we ral - ly 'round the flag, boys, We'll

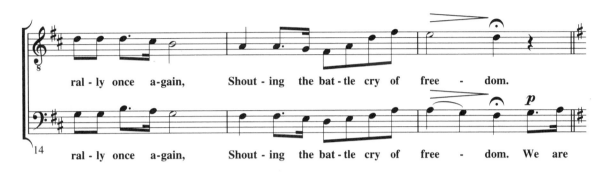

ral - ly once a-gain, Shout - ing the bat - tle cry of free - dom.

ral - ly once a-gain, Shout - ing the bat - tle cry of free - dom. We are

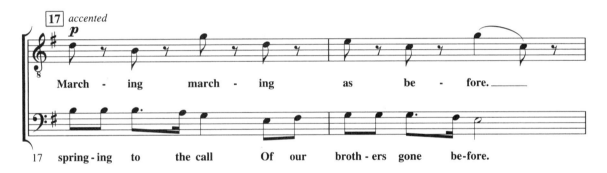

17 *accented*

March - ing march - ing as be - fore._____

spring - ing to the call Of our broth - ers gone be - fore.

Shout - ing that bat - tle cry of free - dom; March - ing with a

Shout - ing the bat - tle cry of free - dom; And we'll fill the va - cant ranks With a

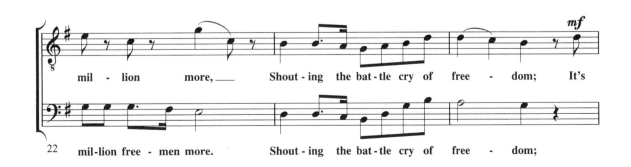

mil - lion more,____ Shout - ing the bat - tle cry of free - dom; It's

mil-lion free - men more. Shout - ing the bat - tle cry of free - dom;

freedom forever, hurrah, boys, hurrah; Down with the shackle and

Free-dom for-ev-er, Free-dom, hur-rah; Down with the shack-le,

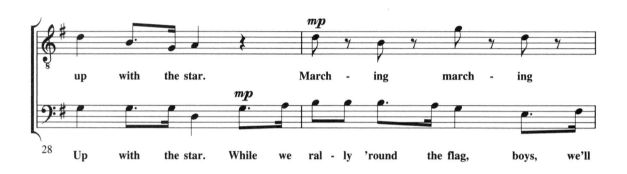

up with the star. March - ing march - ing

Up with the star. While we ral - ly 'round the flag, boys, we'll

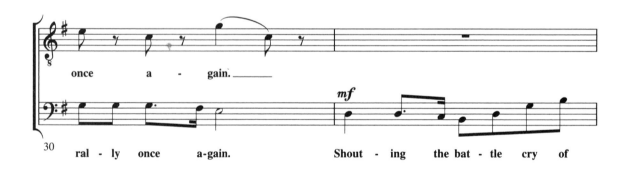

once a - gain. _____

ral - ly once a-gain. Shout - ing the bat - tle cry of

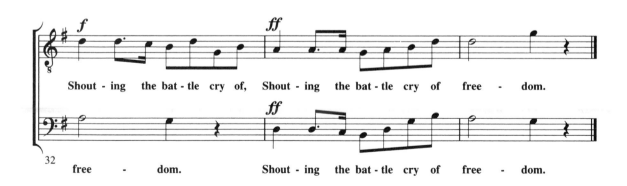

Shout - ing the bat - tle cry of, Shout - ing the bat - tle cry of free - dom.

free - dom. Shout - ing the bat - tle cry of free - dom.

 **SPOTLIGHT**

Careers In Music

Teacher

Music teachers share their love of music with their students. To teach music in a public school, you must have a bachelor's degree in music education. That will require at least four years of college, including one semester of student teaching. High school and junior high music teachers usually specialize in one performance area such as choir, band or orchestra. They may also teach general music, music theory, music appreciation, keyboard and guitar. Elementary music teachers enjoy working with young children. Their job is varied in that they teach singing, dancing, how to play instruments, listening, world music and much more.

At the college level, a music professor must have additional training. Although the minimum requirement is to have a master's degree in music, most colleges require you to have a doctorate as well. College professors teach students how to become professional musicians and professional teachers.

Some musicians choose to teach music through their church or synagogue. Church musicians may be full-time or part-time employees. They might serve as singers, choir directors, organists, instrumentalists or **cantors** *(people who sing and teach music in temples or synagogues)*. Some of these positions require a college degree in music.

Private studio teachers enjoy working with students on a one-on-one basis. They teach from their homes, from private studios, or sometimes at schools. Private instructors teach voice, piano/keyboard, or any of the musical instruments. Their hours are flexible, but they often work in the evenings or weekends because that is when their students are not in school.

Come Travel With Me

Composer: Scott Farthing
Text: Walt Whitman
Voicing: TTB

VOCABULARY

dynamics

triplet

ritardando

a tempo

trio

 SPOTLIGHT

To learn more about posture, see page 13.

Focus

- Identify dynamic markings in music.
- Read and perform rhythmic patterns that contain triplets.
- Relate music to other subjects (poetry).

Getting Started

> *Lets go! Wherever you are, let's go!*
>
> *Come travel with me.*
>
> *Let's go! We must not stop here, let's go!*
>
> *We will not fear!*

The words in a song often create an image in the singer's mind. The text or poetry plays a very important role in making the song come alive. Read the words above. Who do you think is telling the story, and to whom is he speaking? The traveler encourages the reader to explore, travel and face the journey of life not with fear, but with a sense of joyful abandon.

◆ History and Culture

American poet Walt Whitman (1819–1892) is considered one of the world's major literary leaders. "Leaves of Grass," published in 1892, contains over 300 poems. It is interesting to note that many of Whitman's poems contain musical references of some type and that he felt music was an inspiration to his writing.

The text of "Come Travel With Me" is loosely based on Walt Whitman's famous poem "Song of the Open Road." In this poem, Whitman shares with the readers his overwhelming zest for life and his appreciation for the world around him. The music and adaptation of words to "Come Travel With Me" were written in 2001 by Scott Farthing, who at the time was a high school choral director in the Kansas City, Missouri, area.

Links to Learning

◆ Vocal

The **dynamics** (*the symbols in music that indicate how loud or soft to sing*) used in "Come Travel with Me" add expression and interest to the song. Perform the following example with the indicated dynamic markings.

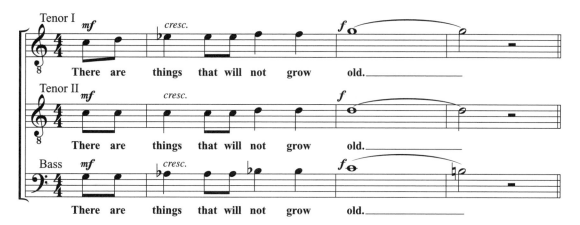

◆ Theory

A **triplet** is *a group of notes in which three notes of equal duration are sung in the time normally given to two notes of equal duration.* A quarter note triplet consists of three quarter notes performed in two beats. Practice the following example to learn how to perform quarter note triplets.

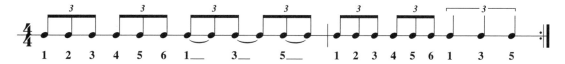

◆ Artistic Expression

In music, tempo markings are used to tell a singer how fast or slow to sing. **Ritardando** (*rit.*) is *a term used to indicate gradually slowing down.* Sometimes following the ritardando is **a tempo,** or *a term used to indicate the return to the original tempo.* Sing measures 10–13 and apply these tempo markings.

Evaluation

Demonstrate how well you have learned the skills and concepts featured in the lesson "Come Travel With Me" by completing the following:

- Make a chart that represents the dynamic markings in this song. In one column, list the boxed measure numbers; in the other column, list the dynamic markings for that section. Check your work with a classmate.

- As a **trio** (*a group of three singers with usually one on a part*), perform measures 21–36 to show that you can read and sing triplets correctly. How well did you do?

For the 2001 National ACDA Junior High Honor Choir
Dr. Lynne Gackle, Conductor

Come Travel With Me

TTB and Piano

Inspired by Walt Whitman's
Song of the Open Road

Words and Music by
SCOTT FARTHING

SPOTLIGHT

Concert Etiquette

The term **concert etiquette** describes *how we are expected to behave in formal musical performances.* Understanding appropriate concert etiquette allows you to be considerate of others, including audience members and performers. It also helps everyone attending to enjoy the performance.

Different types of musical performances dictate certain behavior guidelines. How one shows excitement at a rock concert is certainly worlds apart from the appropriate behavior at a formal concert or theatre production. Understanding these differences allows audience members to behave in a manner that shows consideration and respect for everyone involved.

What are the expectations of a good audience member at a formal musical presentation?

- Arrive on time. If you arrive after the performance has begun, wait outside the auditorium until a break in the music to enter the hall.

- Remain quiet and still during the performance. Talking and moving around prevents others from hearing and enjoying the performance.

- Leave the auditorium only in case of an emergency. Try to leave during a break in the musical selections.

- Sing or clap along only when invited to do so by the performers or the conductor.

- Applaud at the end of a composition or when the conductor lowers his arms at the conclusion of the performance. It is customary to not applaud between movements or sections of a major work.

- Save shouting, whistling and dancing for rock concerts or athletic events. These are never appropriate at formal musical performances.

Remembering these important behavior guidelines will ensure that everyone enjoys the show!

Frog Went A-Courtin'

Composer: Traditional Folk Song, arranged by Audrey Snyder
Text: Traditional
Voicing: TB

VOCABULARY

narrative song

modulation

pentatonic scale

octave

Focus

- Perform music based on the pentatonic scale.
- Use standard terminology to describe octave and unison.
- Perform music that represents an American narrative folk song.

 **SPOTLIGHT**

To learn more about diction, see page 119.

Getting Started

Mickey Mouse®, Donald Duck®, Scooby Doo®, Tom and Jerry®…

Who is your favorite cartoon animal? If the American folk song "Frog Went A-Courtin'" were a cartoon, Frog, Miss Mouse and Uncle Rat would certainly be unforgettable characters. In this story, Frog is courtin' (going out with) Miss Mouse and asks her to marry him. She asks permission from Uncle Rat, who replies, "Marry whom you please." That is a fitting answer for a perfectly silly cartoon story.

◆ History and Culture

"Frog Went A-Courtin'" is a **narrative song,** or *a song that tells a story*. Since the melody remains the same for all eight verses, arranger Audrey Snyder uses **modulation,** or *a change in the key or tonal center of a piece of music within a song*, to create variety. The tonal center or key at the beginning of the song is G major. As the song progresses, it modulates to the key of Ab major and then to A major.

Although this arrangement contains eight verses, other versions have many more verses. In one version, numerous wedding guests are introduced, including a flyin' moth, a juney bug, a bumbley bee, a broken back flea, Mrs. Cow, a little black tick and the old gray cat.

Audrey Snyder has also included several opportunities for you to develop the characters using spoken dialogue and dramatic effects. Have fun singing this well-known narrative folk song.

Links to Learning

◆ Vocal

"Frog Went A-Courtin'" is based on the **pentatonic scale,** *a five-tone scale that contains the pitches* do re, mi, sol, *and* la *of a corresponding major scale.* In a comfortable range for your voice, sing the pentatonic scales as shown for the three key signatures used in this song.

◆ Theory

An **octave** is *an interval of two pitches that are eight notes apart on a staff.* For example, if you were to sing low "G" and someone else were to sing high "G" at the same time, then you would be singing in octaves. On the other hand, if you both were to sing the same note at the same time, then you would be singing in unison. Find examples of singing in octaves and singing in unison in the music.

◆ Artistic Expression

As you sing "Frog Went A-Courtin'," it becomes apparent that the three characters are very animated and full of personality. Using the text and style of the song as your guide, draw Frog, Miss Mouse, and Uncle Rat as cartoon characters.

Evaluation

Demonstrate how well you have learned the skills and concepts featured in the lesson "Frog Went A-Courtin'" by completing the following:

- On a sheet of staff paper, write the notes for a pentatonic scale in three different keys. Sing or play each pattern to check that the notes are correct.

- With a small group, sing verse 7 (measures 104–118) to demonstrate your ability to sing unisons and octaves with clear diction. Ask a classmate to evaluate your performance.

- Make a program cover for "Frog Went A-Courtin'" using your cartoon drawings of the characters. Critique the artwork based on how well it conveys the character and spirit of the song.

Frog Went A-Courtin'

For TB and Piano and Optional Hand Percussion

Arranged by
AUDREY SNYDER

Traditional Folk Song

*The sound of horse hooves; use temple blocks or coconut shells.
**Knock on a piece of wood, or use whatever sounds like a knock on a door.
***May be sung as a solo or by a small group.

*May be sung as a solo or by a small group (sung or spoken in a high voice).

*Pat lap with both hands.

*May be sung as a solo or by a small group.

Guantanamera

Composer: Cuban Folk Song, arranged by John Higgins
Text: Based on the poem "Simple Verses" by José Martí (1853–1895), with English lyrics by John Higgins
Voicing: TB

VOCABULARY

refrain

syllabic stress

SPOTLIGHT

To learn more about vowels, see page 65.

Focus

- Perform Spanish diction with clarity and proper syllabic stress.

- Perform music that represents the Cuban heritage.

- Relate music to history, culture and literature.

Getting Started

Did you know that some songs begin as poems before they are set to music? It is possible that your favorite song started out as a set of written words that did not have a specific melody connected to it. Often, composers will start with an existing poem or text and then set it to music. Such is the case with "Guantanamera."

◆ History and Culture

"Guantanamera" is based on a poem entitled "Simple Verses," written by Cuban writer José Martí. Martí was born in Cuba in 1853. While growing up, Martí had a strong desire that his country would gain its independence. His poetry was inspirational and promoted virtues such as equality among all men, compassion, integrity, love and freedom. Ralph Waldo Emerson and Walt Whitman, famous American poets, admired Martí's writings. After years of exile in New York City, Martí returned to his native Cuba in 1895 and was killed while taking part in the struggle for independence against the Spanish army.

The term *Guantanamera* refers to a girl from the city of Guantanamo, Cuba. The term *guajira* is a colloquial (slang) term for a country girl. Both of these terms are found in the **refrain** (*a repeated section at the end of a verse in a song*). These terms could actually refer to a girl or to the city of Guantanamo itself.

Links to Learning

◆ Vocal

Perform the following example to practice singing with tall uniform vowels and tuning the harmonies found in "Guantanamera."

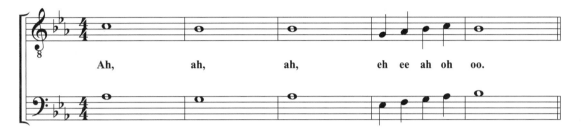

Ah,   ah,   ah,   eh ee ah oh oo.

◆ Theory

Perform the following example by clapping the eighth note pulse at a slow tempo and chanting the rhythmic pattern on the neutral syllable "da."

◆ Artistic Expression

Speak the Spanish text of the piece using proper **syllabic stress,** or *the stressing of one syllable over another.* Stress the syllables that are underlined.

<u>guan</u>-ta-na-<u>me</u>-ra! gua-ji-ra <u>guan</u>-ta-na-<u>me</u>-ra

Yo soy un <u>hom</u>-bre sin-<u>ce</u>-ro de <u>don</u>-de <u>cre</u>-ce la <u>pal</u>-ma

<u>Y</u> <u>an</u>-tes de mor-<u>rir</u>-me <u>quie</u>-ro, e-<u>char</u> mis <u>ver</u>-sos del <u>al</u>-ma

Evaluation

Demonstrate how well you have learned the skills and concepts featured in the lesson "Guantanamera" by completing the following:

- With a partner, take turns chanting the text of "Guantanamera" in Spanish. Evaluate how well you were able to use correct syllabic stress.

- Sing the refrain in Spanish, accurately performing all pitches and rhythms. How well did you do?

- Using the Internet or the library, learn more about José Martí. Write a short introduction about him to be read at a performance of "Guantanamera." What did you learn? How might your introduction enhance the performance of this song?

Guantanamera

For TB and Piano

Cuban Folk Song
Arranged by JOHN HIGGINS

English lyrics by JOHN HIGGINS
Piano Arrangement by DEAN CROCKER

Joshua!
(Fit The Battle Of Jericho)

Composer: Traditional Spiritual, adapted and arranged by Kirby Shaw
Text: Traditional
Voicing: TTB

VOCABULARY

arrangement

imitation

descant

syncopation

improvisation

 SPOTLIGHT

To learn more about improvisation, see page 181.

Focus

- Describe techniques used in creating an arrangement.
- Perform music representing the African American spiritual.

Getting Started

Think of a short simple song from childhood that you know very well. Sing through the song in your head. Once you have done this, add a driving rock beat to the piece and sing the new arrangement in your head. Now add a bass guitar, a lead guitar and a synthesizer to your piece. What does the piece sound like now? If you are amazed by the way you have arranged the piece that is now in your head, wait until you sing Kirby Shaw's arrangement of "Joshua! (Fit The Battle Of Jericho)."

◆ History and Culture

"Joshua! (Fit The Battle Of Jericho)" is a traditional African American spiritual. Taken from Old Testament scripture, the text tells the story of Joshua, an experienced military leader who conquered the city of Jericho. The ancient city of Jericho is considered the oldest known inhabited city in the world.

An **arrangement** is *a song in which a composer takes an existing song and adds extra features.* In this arrangement of "Joshua!," Kirby Shaw has added syncopated rock rhythms, as well as using **imitation** *(the act of one part copying what another part has already sung).* He has also added a **descant** *(a special part that is usually sung higher than the other parts)* and occasional jazz-style harmonies.

Links to Learning

◆ **Vocal**

Read and perform the following example to become familiar with the harmonies and rhythms found in "Joshua! (Fit The Battle Of Jericho)."

◆ **Theory**

Some of the syncopated rhythms in this piece are quite interesting. **Syncopation** is *the placement of accents on a weak beat or a weak portion of the beat.* Clap, chant and step the following rhythmic patterns. Repeat as desired.

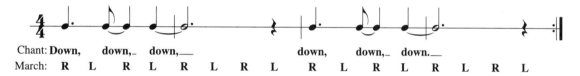

Chant: **Down,   down,_   down,___   down,   down,_   down.___**
March: R   L   R   L   R   L   R   L   R   L   R   L   R   L   R   L

◆ **Artistic Expression**

Improvisation is *the art of singing or playing music, making it up as you go.* It is often used in the performance of spirituals. After you know the song well, try singing an improvisational descant in measures 59–67.

Evaluation

Demonstrate how well you have learned the skills and concepts featured in the lesson "Joshua! (Fit The Battle Of Jericho)" by completing the following:

• Define and locate in the music examples of descant, imitation and syncopation. Describe how they were used to create this arrangement.

• Perform an improvised descant in measures 59–67 in the style of the piece. Critique your improvisation based on your ability to keep in the style of the piece and how well your improvisation complemented the other parts.

Joshua!
(Fit The Battle Of Jericho)

For TTB and Piano

Adapted and Arranged by
KIRBY SHAW

Traditional Spiritual

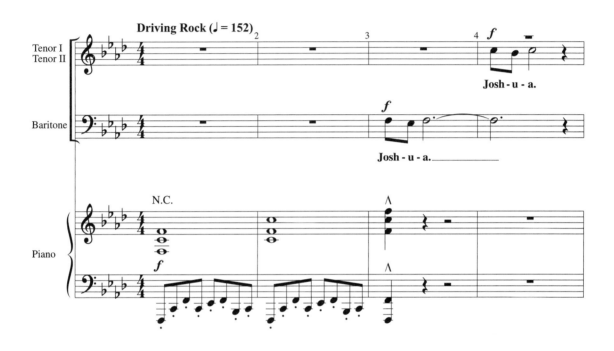

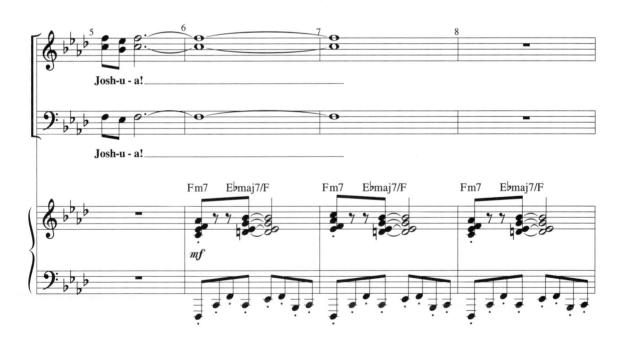

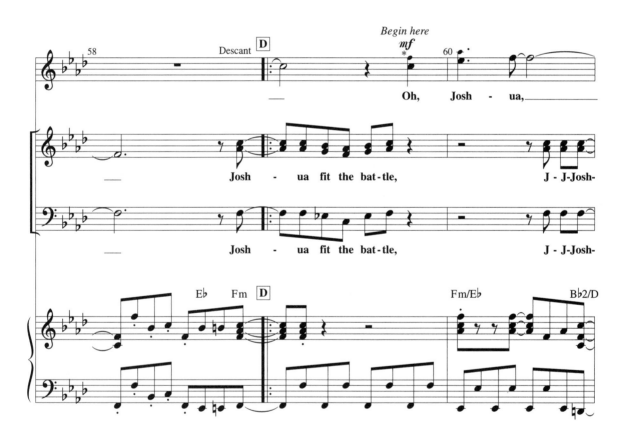

*Cued notes - sing upper or lower notes, not both.

SPOTLIGHT

Breath Management

Vocal sound is produced by air flowing between the vocal cords; therefore, correct breathing is important for good singing. Good breath management provides you with the support needed to sing expressively and for longer periods of time.

To experience, explore and establish proper breathing for singing:

- Put your hands on your waist at the bottom of your rib cage.

- Take in an easy breath for four counts, as if through a straw, without lifting your chest or shoulders.

- Feel your waist and rib cage expand all the way around like an inflating inner tube.

- Let your breath out slowly on "sss," feeling your "inner tube" deflating as if it has a slow leak.

- Remember to keep your chest up the entire time.

- Take in another easy breath for four counts before your "inner tube" has completely deflated, then let your air out on "sss" for eight counts.

- Repeat this step several times, taking in an easy breath for four counts and gradually increasing the number of counts to let your air out to sixteen counts.

Sometimes in singing it is necessary to take a quick or "catch" breath.

- Look out the window and imagine seeing something wonderful for the first time, like snow.

- Point your finger at the imaginary something and let in a quick, silent breath that expresses your wonderment and surprise.

- A quick breath is not a gasping breath, but rather a silent breath.

Leave Her, Johnny

Composer: Traditional Sea Chantey, arranged by Emily Crocker
Text: Traditional
Voicing: TB/TTB

VOCABULARY

sea chantey

staggered
 breathing

dissonance

Focus

- Sing phrases expressively using staggered breathing.
- Identify and describe the music terminology for dissonance.
- Relate music to writing (poetry and short stories).

 **SPOTLIGHT**

To learn more about vocal production, see page 215.

Getting Started

"Leave Her, Johnny" is another example of a **sea chantey,** or *a song sung by sailors, usually in rhythm with their work.* Although it appears from the title that this is a song about a sailor who must leave his girlfriend, quite the opposite is true. The story is about a sailor leaving his ship ("her") to get married ("tomorrow is your wedding day") to his girlfriend back home.

◆ History and Culture

When researching most sea chanteys, you can find many versions of the same song. This is also true for "Leave Her, Johnny." This song was traditionally sung as the sailors came to port. One can only imagine how anxious the sailors were to leave the ship after many months at sea. The sailors would make up verses to "Leave Her, Johnny" to complain about unpleasant conditions aboard the ship. Perhaps the food had been terrible or the work especially hard. Singing has always been a good way to feel better about your problems.

After you are familiar with this song, try composing a new verse about a good reason to be back in port. As is customary in chanteys, do not change the words in the second or fourth line. "Leave her, Johnny, leave her" and "It's time for us to leave her" should be sung in every verse.

Links to Learning

◆ Vocal

To perform "Leave Her, Johnny" with a continuous, flowing melodic line, it is necessary to use **staggered breathing** (*the practice of planning breaths so that no two singers take a breath at the same time*). This song should be sung in four-bar phrases without a noticeable break in between. With a partner who sings your voice part, plan the breaths so that each four-bar phrase sounds continuous.

◆ Theory

Dissonance is *a combination of pitches that clash.* Read and perform the following examples to train your ears to hear and recognize dissonance.

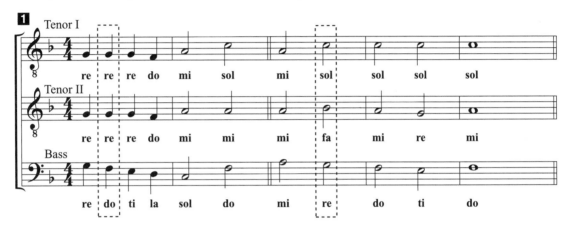

◆ Artistic Expression

The storyteller sings, "The trip was hard and the wind was strong." What events made the trip hard? Imagine you are that sailor long ago. Write a story to your family back home about your adventures on the open seas.

Evaluation

Demonstrate how well you have learned the skills and concepts featured in the lesson "Leave Her, Johnny" by completing the following:

- With a partner, perform "Leave Her, Johnny" and plan the staggered breathing. Evaluate how well you were able to create a continuous, flowing line.

- Listen to a recording of "Leave Her, Johnny." Identify the places where dissonance occurs by raising your hand each time you hear it. How well did you do?

Leave Her, Johnny

For TB or TTB, a cappella

Arranged by
EMILY CROCKER

Traditional Sea Chantey

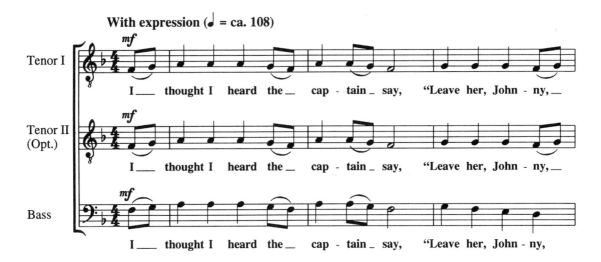

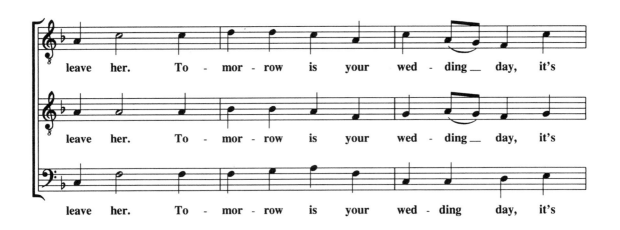

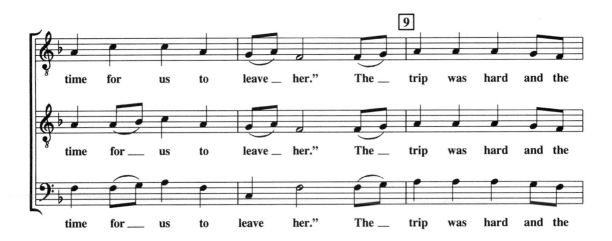

wind was __ strong, Leave her, John - ny, __ leave her. But

wind was __ strong, Leave her, John - ny, __ leave her. But

wind was __ strong, Leave her, John - ny, leave her. But

you'll be back be - fore e'er __ long, It's time for us to

you'll be back be - fore e'er __ long, It's time for __ us to

you'll be back be - fore e'er long, It's time for __ us to

leave __ her. It's __ time for us to leave her.

leave __ her. It's __ time for us to leave __ her.

leave her. It's __ time for us to leave __ her.

New River Train

Composer: American Spiritual, arranged by Donald Moore
Text: Traditional, with additional words by Donald Moore
Voicing: TB

VOCABULARY

syncopation

scale

major scale

Focus

- Identify standard music symbols for rhythm.

- Sight-sing music.

- Relate music to history.

 **SKILL BUILDERS**

*To learn more about
the key of F major,
see* Intermediate Sight-
Singing, *page 39.*

Getting Started

"New River Train" is a fun song to learn and perform because it is very rhythmic. This song repeatedly features syncopated rhythms. **Syncopation** is *the placement of accents on a weak beat or a weak portion of the beat.* The syncopated pattern first appears in measure 5 on the words "ridin' that." Notice that the strong syllable in the word "ridin'" falls off the beat. Again in measure 15, a rest falls on beat 1. This beat of silence brings attention to the syncopated word "brought." When performing "New River Train," accent the syncopated syllables to draw attention to the syncopated rhythm.

◆ History and Culture

The lyrics of many spirituals refer to going home. The mode of transportation in "New River Train" is no longer a horse-drawn chariot, but a steam-engine train! A British inventor named Stephen Trevithick is credited with building the first operational steam locomotive at the beginning of the nineteenth century. The earliest trains were created to haul coal out of mines, but in 1825, the first public passenger railway opened in England. About the same time, trains started to be built in America. By 1835, over a thousand miles of track had been laid, mostly on the East Coast. Trains played a very important role in the westward expansion of the United States throughout the 1880s, capturing the imagination of a nation. So it's natural that trains entered into song lyrics.

Links to Learning

◆ Vocal

This song is in the key of F major and is based on the F major scale. A **scale** is *a group of notes that are sung in succession and are based on a particular keynote, or home tone.* A **major scale** is *a scale that has* do *as its keynote, or home tone.* To locate "F" on a piano, find any set of three black keys. "F" is the white key to the left of the bottom black key. This scale uses the notes F, G, A, B♭, C, D, E, F. Using the keyboard below as a guide, play the F major scale.

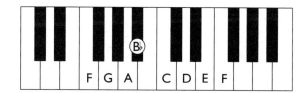

Sing the F major scale in the octave that best fits your voice.

◆ Theory

Learning to sight-sing aids in learning new music faster. Follow this procedure to learn to sight-sing. Look at measures 68–95. First use counting syllables to chant the rhythms. When the rhythms are correct, chant these as solfège syllables. Sight-sing the pitches. Even if you make a mistake, keep going! Identify sections that are repeated. Sing your part on solfège syllables or a neutral syllable, and then add the lyrics. Repeat this process as you learn new music.

Evaluation

Demonstrate how well you have learned the skills and concepts featured in the lesson "New River Train" by completing the following:

- Locate in the music examples of syncopation in your part. Remember that notes or rests can be used to place accented syllables on the weak portion of a beat. Share your examples with a classmate and, together, decide how well you were able to identify syncopation in the music.

- Individually sing measures 27–59 to demonstrate your ability to sight-sing music using correct rhythms and pitches. Based on this criteria, rate your performance on a scale of 1 to 5, with 5 being the best.

New River Train

For TB and Piano

Arranged with Additional Words and Music by
DONALD MOORE

American Spiritual

* The accompaniment should simulate the rhythmic sound of a moving train.

brought me here, gon - na car - ry me home a - gain.___

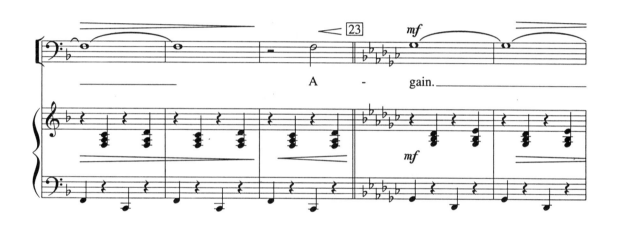

A - gain.___

I'm rid - in' that new riv - er train.___

gain,_____ gon - na car - ry me home a - gain._____

home a - gain, gon - na car - ry me home a - gain._____

50

_____ Home a - gain, home a - gain,_____ gon - na

Home a - gain, home a - gain, gon - na

car - ry me home a - gain._____

car - ry me home a - gain._____

mp

home a - gain,_____ gon - na car - ry me home a -

gain,_____ home a - gain, gon - na car - ry me home a -

96

sub. mp   *mf* ——— *f* ———

gain.   Rid - in' that new,   rid - in' that new,

mf ——— *f*

gain.   Rid - in' that new,_____

96

sub. mp   *mf* ——— *f*

ff

new riv - er train._____

ff

new riv - er train._____

ff

SPOTLIGHT

Improvisation

Improvisation is *the art of singing or playing music, making it up as you go.* **Scat singing** is *an improvisational style of singing that uses nonsense syllables instead of words.* Sometimes, these nonsense sounds can imitate the sound of an instrument. Scat singing, especially as a solo, can be the scariest part of singing jazz.

Dr. Kirby Shaw, one of the top vocal jazz composers and conductors in the world today, offers some suggestions to help build your confidence in this fun and exciting art form.

Start your scat solo with a short melodic or rhythmic idea from the tune being performed. There is nothing wrong in having a preconceived idea before starting to sing a scat solo! By gradually developing the idea as you sing, you will have an organized solo that sounds completely improvised.

Start with scat syllables like "doo" when singing swing tunes. Try "bee," "dee," and "dn" for occasional accented eighth notes on the *and* of beats (1 *and* 2 *and* 3 *and* 4 *and*). Try "doot" or "dit" for short last notes of a musical phrase.

Be able to imitate any sound you like from the world around you, such as a soft breeze, a car horn or a musical instrument. There might be a place for that sound in one of your solos.

Listen to and imitate, note-for-note, the great jazz singers or instrumentalists. You can be inspired by musicians like Ella Fitzgerald, Jon Hendricks, Louis Armstrong or Charlie Parker.

Learn to sing the blues. You can listen to artists like B. B. King, Stevie Ray Vaughan, Buddy Guy or Luther Allison. There are many types of recordings from which to choose.

In short, learn as many different kinds of songs as you can. The best scat singers quote from such diverse sources as nursery rhymes, African chant and even opera. Above all, have fun as you develop your skills!

On The Deep, Blue Sea

Composer: Mary Donnelly, arranged by George L. O. Strid
Text: Mary Donnelly
Voicing: TTB

VOCABULARY

sea chantey

chanteyman

chord

cut time

SKILL BUILDERS

To learn more about cut time, see Intermediate Sight-Singing, *page 140.*

Focus

- Describe and perform chords in tune.
- Sing expressively in a spirited style.
- Read rhythms in cut time.

Getting Started

Have you ever played a game to make the time go by faster? Maybe you've played "I Spy" while traveling by car, or maybe you sang a counting song such as "This Old Man." The song "On The Deep, Blue Sea" is a newly composed piece patterned after **sea chanteys,** *songs sung by sailors, usually in the rhythm of their work.* Singing songs such as this would make the time pass more quickly and raise the sailors' spirits!

◆ History and Culture

Sailors have sung songs of the sea for centuries. The rhythmic flow of the songs helped sailors perform the repetitive jobs while aboard ships. There are two broad categories of sea chanteys based on types of work done.

Hauling chantey – Sung when hauling ropes

Capstan chantey – Sung when raising heavy weights such as the ship's anchor

"On The Deep, Blue Sea" is written in the style of a hauling chantey.

A **chanteyman** was *a soloist who improvised and led the singing of sea chanteys.* He would sing the verses of a chantey and the other sailors would join in on the chorus. A chanteyman was hired with care; his abilities to improvise verses and inspire the men were of prime importance to the captain. The chanteyman was often excused from the heavy work aboard the ship.

Links to Learning

◆ Vocal

A **chord** (*the combination of three or more notes played together at the same time*) is used to make harmony. Practice the following chords to develop the skill of singing in harmony.

◆ Theory

"On The Deep, Blue Sea" is written in **cut time** meter, *a time signature in which there are two beats per measure and the half note receives the beat.* Read and perform the following example to feel the pulse of two beats per measure.

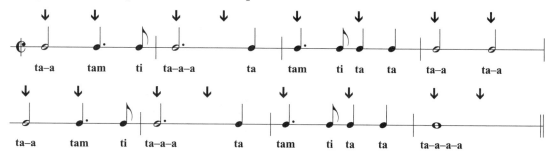

◆ Artistic Expression

Contrasts in style give a song interest and variety. In verse 2 (measures 39–55), each section of the choir is featured. Use word stress to add character to the text and strive to make your part the most expressive. Verse 3 (measures 74–90) is more dramatic. The changes in tempo will allow you to be creative in your presentation.

Evaluation

Demonstrate how well you have learned the skills and concepts featured in the lesson "On The Deep, Blue Sea" by completing the following:

- With a small group, perform measures 29–37. Evaluate how well you were able to sing the chords in tune and create harmony.

- Chant the words to verse 2 (measures 74–90) expressively. Exaggerate the changes in tempo, mood and expression. Then sing the verse. In what ways did you perform the verse differently after chanting the words expressively?

On The Deep, Blue Sea

For TTB and Piano

Arranged by
GEORGE L. O. STRID (ASCAP)

Words and Music by
MARY DONNELLY (ASCAP)

las-sie with her smile so sweet. She'll tell you that she loves you, then

las-sie with her smile so sweet. She'll tell you that she loves you, then

las-sie with her smile so sweet. She'll tell you that she loves you, then

ask you for a wed-ding ring, and then she'll tie an an-chor chain a-round your

ask you for a wed-ding ring, and then she'll tie an an-chor chain a-round your

ask you for a wed-ding ring, and then she'll tie an an-chor chain a-round your

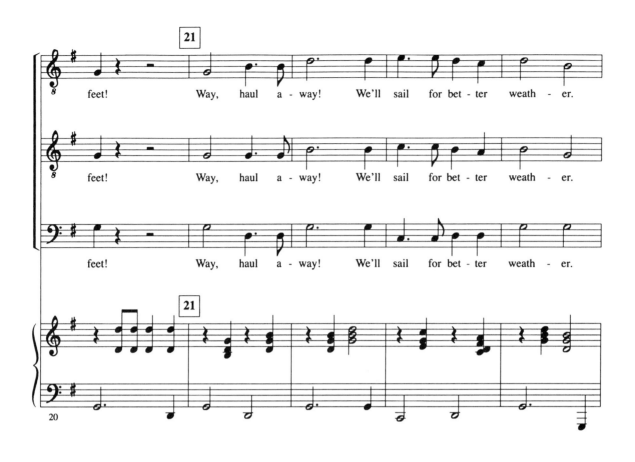

way! We'll sail the waves for - ev – er. There's free-dom and ad - ven-ture on the

way! We'll sail the waves for - ev – er. There's free-dom and ad - ven-ture on the

way! We'll sail the waves for - ev – er. There's free-dom and ad - ven-ture on the

30

deep, blue sea._____

deep, blue sea._____

deep, blue sea._____

A

35

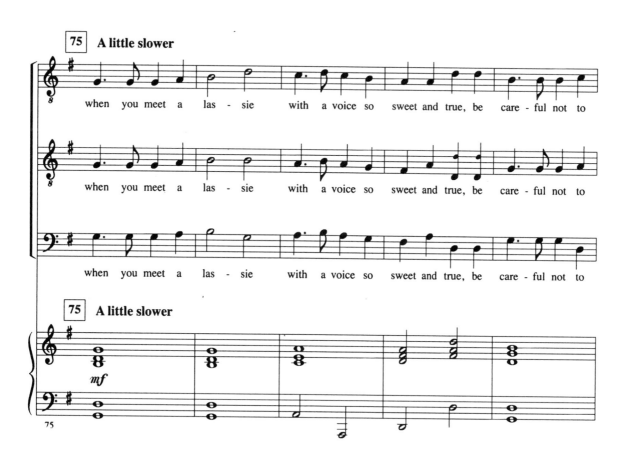

SPOTLIGHT

Changing Voice

As we grow in size and maturity, we don't always grow at the same rate. Just look around your school or neighborhood. Some thirteen-year-olds tower over other students, while some are quite small.

As the voice matures, it changes in both pitch and **timbre** *(tone quality).* The vocal folds or cords are growing longer and thicker. Just like growing in stature, this process is not the same for every person. One person's voice might drop an octave almost overnight, while another person's changes very gradually.

The Male Voice

While every voice change is unique, male singers usually progress through several identifiable stages:

- Before the voice begins to change, the boy's voice has a very light vocal quality, and the tone is pure and clear. Also, the voice is very flexible with the ability to sing in a high range.

- The first sign of voice change is the loss of clarity and richness in the higher pitches. There is a slight decrease in flexibility due to the growth of the vocal folds or cords. As the voice begins to change or mature, the singer will notice that he loses more notes in his top range than he gains in his new, lower voice.

- As the voice lowers, the quality becomes thicker, huskier and sometimes breathy. There may be signs of hoarseness and breaks in the voice when speaking or singing. The voice appears to be weaker and less flexible. Although the vocal range is limited, this is a temporary stage. The more the singer sings during this time, the easier the transition will be. Also, if a singer will continue to sing in his upper range, it will strengthen the vocal cords and help maintain flexibility in the voice.

- As the voice matures, the lower pitches in the speaking voice become evident. The singing voice is lower, firm and clear.

- When the voice has reached full maturity, it has a thicker, heavier voice quality. The tone is consistent. A male singer can move more easily between the lower and upper registers of his voice, including **falsetto** *(the light upper range of the male voice that extends beyond the natural voice).* The voice will eventually settle into a classification called **tenor** *(the highest-sounding male voice)* or **bass** *(the lowest-sounding male voice).*

Pretty Saro

Composer: American Folk Song, arranged by Jennifer B. Scoggin
Text: Traditional
Voicing: TTB

VOCABULARY

folk song

pentatonic scale

$\frac{3}{4}$ meter

Focus

- Read music notation in $\frac{3}{4}$ meter.
- Write a pentatonic scale.
- Perform music representing American folk music.

Getting Started

Songs quite often tell a story. What is the story behind this song?

"Down in some lone valley in a lonesome place"

Where is this place? Why is it so lonely? Who else is there?

"Farewell pretty Saro, I bid you adieu."

Why did someone have to say good-bye? Who is pretty Saro?

This American folk song is a story waiting to be told. Finish your story by giving your characters names, ages and circumstances. How will this information change the way you perform this song?

 **SKILL BUILDERS**

To learn more about $\frac{3}{4}$ meter, see Intermediate Sight-Singing, *page 17.*

◆ History and Culture

Folk songs are an important part of every culture. They can tell stories of great loves, legends and leaders. **Folk songs** are *songs that are passed down from generation to generation through oral tradition.* They may change with each new generation as each adds its own variation. Make a list of other folk songs you know.

In the early 1900s, many American scholars began to systematically collect and record our folk song literature. Two of our most famous folk song collectors were John and Alan Lomax, a father-and-son team. In 1911 John Lomax published a collection of songs from the Appalachian Mountains. "Pretty Saro" was part of this early collection. Much of the music from Appalachia was handed down from Scottish and Irish ancestors. However, "Pretty Saro" has a third verse that mentions that the girl wants a "freeholder who owns house and land." The term *freeholder* indicates a possible British origin.

Links to Learning

◆ Vocal

A **pentatonic scale** is *a scale based on five pitches (do, re, mi, sol, la).* Notice that in the pentatonic scale the pitches *fa* and *ti* are not used. A pentatonic scale can start on any pitch. For example, the *do* pentatonic scale consists of *do, re, mi, fa, sol.* A *re* pentatonic scale consists of *re, mi, sol, la, do* and so forth. Read and perform the following pentatonic scale to prepare you to sing "Pretty Saro." Sing in the range that best fits your voice.

◆ Theory

"Pretty Saro" is written in $\frac{3}{4}$ **meter,** *a time signature in which there are three beats per measure and the quarter note receives the beat.* Read and perform the following rhythmic patterns to establish $\frac{3}{4}$ meter.

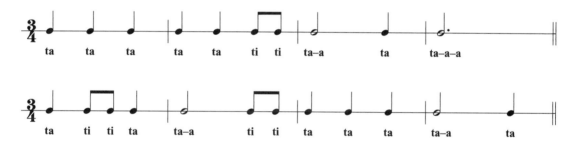

Evaluation

Demonstrate how well you have learned the concepts and skills presented in the lesson "Pretty Saro" by completing the following:

- With a classmate, chant the rhythm and conduct measures 5–20 to show your ability to read music in $\frac{3}{4}$ meter. Critique each other's performance, and identify areas that need improvement.

- Describe a pentatonic scale. On staff paper or on the computer, write a G pentatonic scale beginning on *do.* Sing the scale that you wrote. How well did you do?

Pretty Saro

For TTB and Piano

Arranged by
JENNIFER B. SCOGGIN

American Folk Song

wild birds do whis - tle and their notes do — in - crease. Fare -

well pret - ty — Sa - ro, I bid you a - dieu, But I'll

go.

rit.

pp

Ped.

Santa Lucia

Composer: Teodoro Cottrau (1827–1879), arranged by Henry Leck
Text: Teodoro Cottrau
Voicing: TB

VOCABULARY

barcarole

$\frac{3}{8}$ meter

rubato

Focus

- Read and perform rhythmic patterns in $\frac{3}{8}$ meter.
- Sing expressively using rubato.
- Perform music that represents the Neopolitan barcarole.

 **SKILL BUILDERS**

To learn more about $\frac{3}{8}$ meter, see Intermediate Sight-Singing, *page 154.*

Getting Started

What do these three songs have in common? How are they different?

"You Gentlemen Of England" (see page 216)

"On The Deep, Blue Sea" (see page 182)

"Santa Lucia" (see page 204)

Share your answers with your classmates. It is interesting to see how different cultures express similar ideas through music.

◆ History and Culture

Italian songwriter Teodoro Cottrau (1827–1879) wrote 50 Neapolitan songs, of which "Santa Lucia" is perhaps his most famous. Written in 1850, "Santa Lucia" is an example of a **barcarole**, *a Venetian boating song.* Over the years, it has become the anthem of Naples, Italy, and a favorite among tenors. Cottrau was also a music publisher, lawyer, poet and politician.

"Santa Lucia" is a very popular song with the gondoliers who guide the gondolas (long narrow boats) through the water canals of Venice, Italy. The music expresses the joy of being out in the sea breezes and feeling the flow of the water. It should be sung with a very full and lyric sound, taking liberty with the dynamics and phrasing. While "Santa Lucia" can be sung in English, it is fun and more authentic to sing it in its original language, Italian. Have fun learning this famous Italian boating song.

Links to Learning

◆ Theory

"Santa Lucia" is written in $\frac{3}{8}$ **meter,** *a time signature in which there is one group of three eighth notes per measure and the dotted quarter note receives the beat.* When the tempo is very slow, this meter can be counted as having three beats per measure, with the eighth note receiving the beat.

At the performance tempo, this song should be felt in one. To learn the difference between feeling "Santa Lucia" in one versus three, perform the following examples, first at a slow tempo, feeling the pulse in three. Then repeat the example at the performance tempo, feeling the pulse in one.

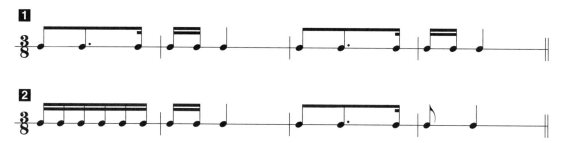

◆ Artistic Expression

Rubato, or *the freedom to slow down and/or speed up the tempo without changing the overall pulse of a piece of music,* is an artistic device that is effective in the performance of "Santa Lucia." Look at the music. Where would you use rubato?

Evaluation

Demonstrate how well you have learned the skills and concepts featured in the lesson "Santa Lucia" by completing the following:

- Alone or in a small group, clap the rhythms in measures 25–32. Check your performance for showing a clear distinction between the eighth note and sixteenth note patterns.

- Select one person to come forward and serve as a "rubato leader." As a class, perform "Santa Lucia," following the leader. How well was the class able to follow the leader?

Santa Lucia

For TB and Piano*

Arranged by
HENRY LECK

Words and Music by
TEODORO COTTRAU (1827–1879)

*Accompaniment CD has a four-measure introduction.

Sing To The Lord

Composer: Emily Crocker
Text: Based on the Psalms
Voicing: TTB

VOCABULARY

ABA form

unison

part-singing

Focus

- Distinguish between unison singing and part-singing.
- Read and perform rhythmic patterns that contain dotted quarter notes.
- Relate music to other subjects.

Getting Started

A Japanese haiku is a form of poetry that uses seventeen syllables of text divided into three lines. Commonly, the first line consists of five syllables, the second seven, and the last five. In describing the subject matter, the poem should also reflect the Japanese philosophy of lightness, simplicity, openness and depth.

Have you ever written a poem? Complete this haiku.

Voices resounding

All joined together as one

Singing, _____ _____ _____.

SPOTLIGHT

To learn more about the dotted quarter notes, see Intermediate Sight-Singing, *page 45.*

◆ History and Culture

Although not written in the style of a haiku, the text to "Sing to the Lord" is poetry. It is loosely based on Psalm 150 and describes singing as jubilant and joyful. Just as there are many different ways to write poetry, there are many different ways to write music. The music to "Sing To The Lord" is written in ABA form. **ABA form** is *the design in which the opening phrase (section A) is followed by a contrasting phrase (section B), which leads to a repetition of the opening phrase (section A).* The opening eight measures beginning with "Sing to the Lord" is section A. Find where section A appears again. The contrasting middle section B ("Praise Him with sounding brass") is different in texture, style and phrasing. By discovering the form or organization of the music, you will find that learning a song may become easier. For example, once you have learned the opening eight measures of "Sing To The Lord," you will already know two-thirds of the song!

Links to Learning

◆ Vocal

In "Sing To The Lord," the choir often sings in **unison** (*all parts singing the same notes*), then moves into **part-singing** (*two or more parts singing an independent line at the same time*), and finally returns to unison singing. Perform the following example to practice moving between unison singing and part-singing. Listen carefully to match the unison pitches.

◆ Theory

A **dot** is *a symbol that increases the length of a given note by half its value.* It is placed to the right of the note. A dotted quarter note receives one and a half beats. Read and perform the following rhythmic patterns that contain dotted quarter notes.

Evaluation

Demonstrate how well you have learned the skills and concepts featured in the lesson "Sing To The Lord" by completing the following:

- Locate in the music (measures 1–8) the places where the voice parts are singing in unison. In a trio with one singer on a part, sing measures 1–8 and hold the unison notes. Evaluate how well your group was able to match pitch on the unison notes.

- Sing measures 1–7 to show your ability to read music that contains dotted quarter notes. Rate your performance on a scale of 1 to 5, with 5 being the best.

Sing To The Lord

For TTB, a cappella

Based on the Psalms

Words and Music by
EMILY CROCKER

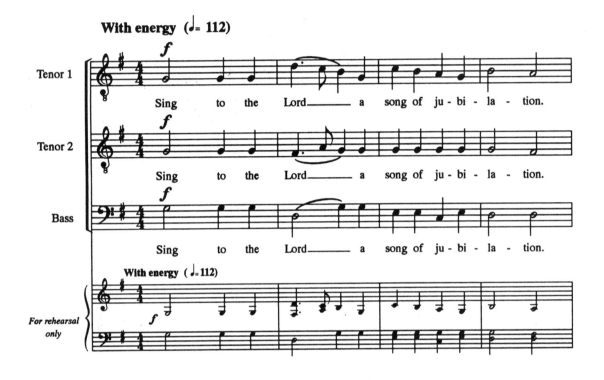

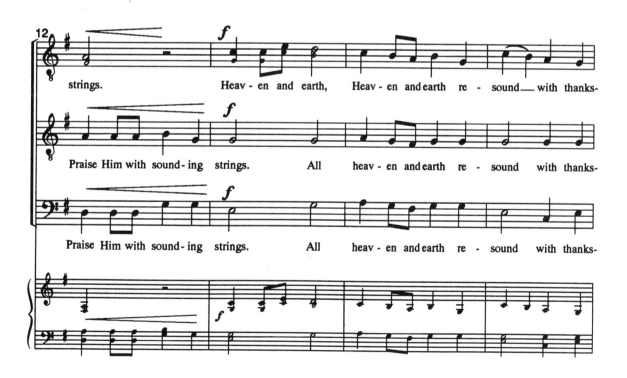

giv - ing. Sing to the Lord_____ a song of ju - bi -

giv - ing. Sing to the Lord_____ a song of ju - bi -

giv - ing. Sing to the Lord_____ a song of ju - bi -

la - tion. Sing to the Lord_____ a song_____ of joy.

la - tion. Sing to the Lord_____ a song of_____ joy.

la - tion. Sing to the Lord_____ a song of_____ joy.

SPOTLIGHT

Vocal Production

There are many ways we can use our voices to communicate. We can speak, shout, laugh, whisper, sigh and sing. This lesson will focus on your singing voice. It is best to think of singing as extended speech so you do not put too much physical effort into it.

Perform the following exercises to experience, explore and establish singing as extended speech.

- Say the phrase "Hello, my name is _____" as if you were greeting someone enthusiastically.

- Say the phrase again, but speak all of it on the same pitch as the first syllable.

- Repeat the phrase, making sure you take a singer's breath before you start.

- Feel the flow of the breath as it smoothly connects each word to the next.

- Try the phrase several times, starting on different pitches, seeing how long you can hold out your name.

- Remember to keep your chest high and your "inner tube" inflated for as long as you can. (It will feel like a belt is tightening around your waist the longer you hold it.)

Explore your **head voice** (*the singer's higher singing voice*) and your **chest voice** (*the singer's lower singing voice*) by performing the following exercises.

- Place your upper teeth on your lower lip as if you were going to say the letter "v."

- Make a singing tone on a lower pitch for a few seconds, keeping your teeth on your lower lip.

- Now, take a singer's breath and start the "v" sound on a lower pitch, but immediately move the pitch upward as high as you can go.

- Repeat the last step, this time bringing the voice back down low again.

- Notice the stretching feeling you have in your throat as you go higher and lower.

You Gentlemen Of England

Composer: Time of Elizabeth, arranged by Barry Talley
Text: Martin Packer
Voicing: TB

VOCABULARY

dynamics

sequence

contrary motion

Focus

- Perform expressively from memory.
- Interpret music symbols referring to dynamics when performing.
- Define musical symbols and writing techniques found in music.

 SPOTLIGHT

To learn more about concert etiquette, see page 137.

Getting Started

The dates April 14, 1912, and September 1, 1985, are linked in history. The first is the day that the ocean liner Titanic sank, and the second is the day that explorers found the wrecked ship located about 2.5 miles beneath the surface of the waters far off the coast of Newfoundland. Rumored to be an unsinkable ship, the Titanic serves as a reminder that life at sea can be both adventurous and dangerous. The lyrics in "You Gentlemen Of England" ask those "who live at home at ease" to remember those who experience "the danger of the seas."

◆ History and Culture

The tune of "You Gentlemen Of England" dates from the time of England's Queen Elizabeth I, who ruled from 1558 to 1603. Like her father, the popular King Henry VIII, she was musically gifted and had a passion for the arts. Moreover, she was a wise ruler. During her reign, England prospered politically and economically, which created favorable conditions for the arts to flourish. Music was a popular entertainment. A good education included learning to play musical instruments and to compose simple tunes. This era, referred to as the Elizabethan Age, also produced great literature. The most famous author from this time is William Shakespeare.

Links to Learning

◆ Vocal

Sing the following example to practice performing a variety of dynamic levels. **Dynamics** are *symbols used in music that indicate how loud or soft to sing.* The first time, sing *f* (loud or full). Repeat the example several times, singing it *p* (soft), *mp* (medium soft), or *mf* (medium loud). Try it different ways.

◆ Theory

Perform the following example to practice singing a sequence. A **sequence** is *a pattern that, when repeated, starts on a different pitch.* Here, the music for the words "and the fears" is a sequence of "all the cares." Also, notice that on the words "All the" and "and the," the Tenor and Bass parts move in **contrary motion,** *a technique in which one part moves up while the other moves down.*

◆ Artistic Expression

The text in measures 16–19 repeats in measures 20–23. Although the melody remains the same, the dynamics change and the Tenors sing a different harmony part. Locate all the dynamic markings. In rehearsal and in performance, sing the contrasting dynamic markings.

Evaluation

Demonstrate how well you have learned the skills and concepts featured in the lesson "You Gentlemen Of England" by completing the following:

- Sing from memory measures 27–46 to reveal your ability to sing expressively by performing all the dynamics as marked. Evaluate how well you were able to sing expressively.

- Record yourself singing measures 12–23. Listen to the recording and evaluate how well you were able to sing with varied dynamics.

You Gentlemen Of England

For TB and Piano

Arranged by
BARRY TALLEY

Music by **MARTIN PACKER**
Music, time of Elizabeth

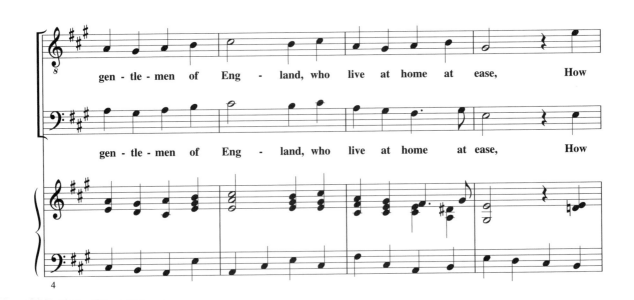

Glossary

CHORAL MUSIC TERMS

2/2 meter   A time signature in which there are two beats per measure and the half note receives the beat.

2/4 meter   A time signature in which there are two beats per measure and the quarter note receives the beat.

3/2 meter   A time signature in which there are three beats per measure and the half note receives the beat.

3/4 meter   A time signature in which there are three beats per measure and the quarter note receives the beat.

3/8 meter   A time signature in which there is one group of three eighth notes per measure and the dotted quarter note receives the beat. When the tempo is very slow, this meter can be counted as having three beats per measure, with the eighth note receiving the beat.

4/4 meter   A time signature in which there are four beats per measure and the quarter note receives the beat.

5/8 meter   A time signature in which there are five beats per measure and the eighth note receives the beat.

6/4 meter   A time signature in which there are two groups of three quarter notes per measure and the dotted half note receives the beat. When the tempo is very slow, this meter can be counted as having six beats per measure, with the quarter note receiving the beat.

6/8 meter   A time signature in which there are two groups of three eighth notes per measure and the dotted quarter note receives the beat. When the tempo is very slow, this meter can be counted as having six beats per measure, with the eighth note receiving the beat.

9/8 meter   A time signature in which there are three groups of three eighth notes per measure and the dotted quarter note receives the beat. When the tempo is very slow, this meter can be counted as having nine beats per measure, with the eighth note receiving the beat.

12/8 meter   A time signature in which there are four groups of three eighth notes per measure and the dotted quarter note receives the beat.

A

a cappella *(ah-kah-PEH-lah)* [It.] A style of singing without instrumental accompaniment.

a tempo *(ah TEM-poh)* [It.] A tempo marking which indicates to return to the original tempo of a piece or section of music.

ABA form   A form in which an opening section (A) is followed by a contrasting section (B), which leads to the repetition of the opening section (A).

accelerando *(accel.) (ah-chel-leh-RAHN-doh)* [It.] A tempo marking that indicates to gradually get faster.

accent   A symbol placed above or below a given note to indicate that the note should receive extra emphasis or stress. ($\overset{>}{\rule{0pt}{6pt}}$)

accidental   Any sharp, flat or natural that is not included in the key signature of a piece of music.

adagio *(ah-DAH-jee-oh)* [It.] Slow tempo, but not as slow as *largo*.

ad libitum *(ad. lib.)* [Lt.] An indication that the performer may vary the tempo or add or delete a vocal or instrumental part.

Aeolian scale *(ay-OH-lee-an)* [Gk.] A modal scale that starts and ends on *la*. It is made up of the same arrangement of whole and half steps as a natural minor scale.

al fine *(ahl FEE-neh)* [It.] To the end.

aleatory music *(AY-lee-uh-toh-ree)* A type of music in which certain aspects are performed randomly. Also known as chance music.

alla breve   Indicates cut time; a duple meter in which there are two beats per measure, and the half note receives the beat. *See* cut time.

allargando (*allarg.*) (*ahl-ahr-GAHN-doh*) [It.] To broaden, become slower.

allegro (*ah-LEH-groh*) [It.] Brisk tempo; faster than *moderato*, slower than *vivace*.

allegro non troppo (*ah-LEH-groh nohn TROH-poh*) [It.] A tempo marking that indicates not too fast. Not as fast as *allegro*.

altered pitch Another name for an accidental.

alto (*AL-toh*) The lowest-sounding female voice.

andante (*ahn-DAHN- teh*) [It.] Moderately slow; a walking tempo.

andante con moto (*ahn-DAHN- teh kohn MOH-toh*) [It.] A slightly faster tempo, "with motion."

animato Quickly, lively; "animated."

anthem A choral composition in English using a sacred text.

arpeggio (*ahr-PEH-jee-oh*) [It.] A chord in which the pitches are sounded successively, usually from lowest to highest; in broken style.

arrangement A piece of music in which a composer takes an existing melody and adds extra features or changes the melody in some way.

arranger A composer who takes an original or existing melody and adds extra features or changes the melody in some way.

art song A musical setting of a poem.

articulation The amount of separation or connection between notes.

articulators The lips, teeth, tongue and other parts of the mouth and throat that are used to produce vocal sound.

avocational Not related to a job or career.

B

barbershop A style of *a cappella* singing in which three parts harmonize with the melody. The lead sings the melody while the tenor harmonizes above and the baritone and bass harmonize below.

barcarole A Venetian boat song.

baritone The male voice between tenor and bass.

barline A vertical line placed on the musical staff that groups notes and rests together.

Baroque period (*bah-ROHK*) [Fr.] The historical period in Western civilization from 1600 to 1750.

bass The lowest-sounding male voice.

bass clef A clef that generally indicates notes that sound lower than middle C.

basso continuo (*BAH-soh cun-TIN-you-oh*) [It.] A continually moving bass line, common in music from the Baroque period.

beat The steady pulse of music.

bebop style Popular in jazz, music that features notes that are light, lively and played quickly. Often the melodic lines are complex and follow unpredictable patterns.

blues scale An altered major scale that uses flatted or lowered third, fifth and seventh notes: *ma* (lowered from *mi*), *se* (lowered from *sol*) and *te* (lowered from *ti*).

blues style An original African American art form that developed in the early twentieth century in the Mississippi Delta region of the South. The lyrics often express feelings of frustration, hardship or longing. It often contains elements such as call and response, the blues scale and swing.

body percussion The use of one's body to make a percussive sound, such as clapping, snapping or stepping.

breath mark A symbol in vocal music used to indicate where a singer should take a breath. (,)

breath support A constant airflow necessary to produce sound for singing.

cadence A melodic or harmonic structure that marks the end of a phrase or the completion of a song.

call and response A derivative of the field hollers used by slaves as they worked. A leader or group sings a phrase (call) followed by a response of the same phrase by another group.

calypso A style of music that originated in the West Indies and which features syncopated rhythms and comical lyrics.

canon A musical form in which one part sings a melody, and the other parts sing the same melody, but enter at different times. Canons are sometimes called rounds.

cantabile (con-TAH-bee-leh) [It.] In a lyrical, singing style.

cantata (con-TAH-tah) [It.] A large-scale musical piece made up of several movements for singers and instrumentalists. Johann Sebastian Bach was a prominent composer of cantatas.

cantor (CAN-tor) A person who sings and/or teaches music in a temple or synagogue.

canzona [It.] A rhythmic instrumental composition that is light and fast-moving.

chamber music Music performed by a small instrumental ensemble, generally with one instrument per part. The string quartet is a popular form of chamber music, consisting of two violins, a viola and a cello. Chamber music was popular during the Classical period.

chantey See sea chantey.

chanteyman A soloist who improvised and led the singing of sea chanteys.

chest voice The lower part of the singer's vocal range.

chorale (kuh-RAL) [Gr.] Congregational song or hymn of the German Protestant Church.

chord The combination of three or more notes played or sung together at the same time.

chromatic scale (kroh-MAT-tick) [Gk.] A scale that consists of all half steps and uses all twelve pitches in an octave.

Classical period The historical period in Western civilization from 1750 to 1820.

clef The symbol at the beginning of a staff that indicates which lines and spaces represent which notes.

coda A special ending to a song. A concluding section of a composition. (⊕)

common time Another name for 4/4 meter. Also known as common meter. (𝄴)

composer A person who takes a musical thought and writes it out in musical notation to share it with others.

compound meter Any meter in which the dotted quarter note receives the beat, and the division of the beat is based on three eighth notes. 6/8, 9/8 and 12/8 are examples of compound meter.

con moto (kohn MOH-toh) [It.] With motion.

concert etiquette A term used to describe what is appropriate behavior in formal or informal musical performances.

concerto (cun-CHAIR-toh) [Fr., It.] A composition for a solo instrument and orchestra.

concerto grosso (cun-CHAIR-toh GROH-soh) [Fr., It.] A multimovement Baroque piece for a group of soloists and an orchestra.

conductor A person who uses hand and arm gestures to interpret the expressive elements of music for singers and instrumentalists.

conductus A thirteenth-century song for two, three or four voices.

consonance Harmonies in chords or music that are pleasing to the ear.

Contemporary period The historical period from 1900 to the present.

countermelody   A separate melodic line that supports and/or contrasts the melody of a piece of music.

counterpoint   The combination of two or more melodic lines. The parts move independently while harmony is created. Johann Sebastian Bach is considered by many to be one of the greatest composers of contrapuntal music.

contrary motion   A technique in which two melodic lines move in opposite directions.

crescendo *(creh-SHEN-doh)*   [It.] A dynamic marking that indicates to gradually sing or play louder. ◁

cut time   Another name for 2/2 meter. (¢)

D

da capo *(D.C.) (dah KAH-poh)*   [It.] Go back to the beginning and repeat; *see* dal segno *and* al fine.

dal segno *(D.S.) (dahl SAYN-yah)*   [It.] Go back to the sign and repeat.

D. C. al Fine *(FEE-nay)*   [It.] A term that indicates to go back to the beginning and repeat. The term *al fine* indicates to sing to the end, or *fine.*

decrescendo *(DAY-creh-shen-doh)*   [It.] A dynamic marking that indicates to gradually sing or play softer. ▷

descant   A special part in a piece of music that is usually sung higher than the melody or other parts of the song.

diatonic scale *(die-uh-TAH-nick)*   A scale that uses no altered pitches or accidentals. Both the major scale and the natural minor scale are examples of a diatonic scale.

diction   The pronunciation of words while singing.

diminished chord   A minor chord in which the top note is lowered one half step from *mi* to *me.*

diminuendo *(dim.) (duh-min-yoo-WEN-doh)*   [It.] Gradually getting softer; *see* decrescendo.

diphthong   A combination of two vowel sounds.

dissonance   A combination of pitches or tones that clash.

dolce *(DOHL-chay)*   [It.] Sweetly.

dominant chord   A chord built on the fifth note of a scale. In a major scale, this chord uses the notes *sol, ti* and *re,* and it may be called the **V** ("five") chord, since it is based on the fifth note of the major scale, or *sol.* In a minor scale, this chord uses the notes *mi, sol* and *ti* (or *mi, si* and *ti*), and it may be called the **v** or **V** ("five") chord, since it is based on the fifth note of the minor scale, or *mi.*

Dorian scale *(DOOR-ee-an)*   [Gk.] A modal scale that starts and ends on *re.*

dot   A symbol that increases the length of a given note by half its value. It is placed to the right of the note.

dotted half note   A note that represents three beats of sound when the quarter note receives the beat. ♩.

double barline   A set of two barlines that indicate the end of a piece or section of music.

D. S. al coda *(dahl SAYN-yoh ahl KOH-dah)*   [It.] Repeat from the symbol (𝄋) and skip to the coda when you see the sign. (⊕)

duet   A group of two singers or instrumentalists.

dynamics   Symbols in music that indicate how loud or soft to sing or play.

E

eighth note   A note that represents one half beat of sound when the quarter note receives the beat. Two eighth notes equal one beat of sound when the quarter note receives the beat. ♪ ♫

eighth rest   A rest that represents one half beat of silence when the quarter note receives the beat. Two eighth rests equal one beat of silence when the quarter note receives the beat. ♪

expressive singing   To sing with feeling.

F

falsetto [It.] The register in the male voice that extends far above the natural voice. The light upper range.

fermata (fur-MAH-tah) [It.] A symbol that indicates to hold a note or rest for longer than its given value. (⌒)

fine (fee-NAY) [It.] A term used to indicate the end of a piece of music.

flat A symbol that lowers the pitch of a given note by one half step.(♭)

folk music Music that passed down from generation to generation through oral tradition. Traditional music that reflects a place, event or a national feeling.

folk song A song passed down from generation to generation through oral tradition. A song that reflects a place, event or a national feeling.

form The structure or design of a musical composition.

forte (FOR-tay) [It.] A dynamic that indicates to sing or play loud. (*f*)

fortissimo (for-TEE-see-moh) [It.] A dynamic that indicates to sing or play very loud. (*ff*)

fugue (FYOOG) A musical form in which the same melody is performed by different instruments or voices entering at different times, thus adding layers of sound.

fusion Music that is developed by the act of combining various types and cultural influences of music into a new style.

G

gospel music Religious music that originated in the African American churches of the South. This music can be characterized by improvisation, syncopation and repetition.

grand staff A staff that is created when two staves are joined together.

grandioso [It.] Stately, majestic.

grave (GRAH-veh) [It.] Slow, solemn.

grazioso (grah-tsee-OH-soh) [It.] Graceful.

Gregorian chant A single, unaccompanied melodic line sung by male voices. Featuring a sacred text and used in the church, this style of music was developed in the Medieval period.

H

half note A note that represents two beats of sound when the quarter note receives the beat.

half rest A rest that represents two beats of silence when the quarter note receives the beat.

half step The smallest distance (interval) between two notes on a keyboard; the chromatic scale is composed entirely of half steps.

harmonic minor scale A minor scale that uses a raised seventh note, *si* (raised from *sol*).

harmonics Small whistle-like tones, or overtones, that are sometimes produced over a sustained pitch.

harmony A musical sound that is formed when two or more different pitches are played or sung at the same time.

head voice The higher part of the singer's vocal range.

homophonic (hah-muh-FAH-nik) [Gk.] A texture where all parts sing similar rhythm in unison or harmony.

homophony (haw-MAW-faw-nee) [Gk.] A type of music in which there are two or more parts with similar or identical rhythms being sung or played at the same time. Also, music in which melodic interest is concentrated in one voice part and may have subordinate accompaniment.

hushed A style marking indicating a soft, whispered tone.

imitation The act of one part copying what another part has already played or sung.

improvisation The art of singing or playing music, making it up as you go, or composing and performing a melody at the same time.

International Phonetic Alphabet (IPA) A phonetic alphabet that provides a notational standard for all languages. Developed in Paris, France in 1886.

interval The distance between two notes.

intonation The accuracy of pitch, in-tune singing.

Ionian scale *(eye-OWN-ee-an)* [Gk.] A modal scale that starts and ends on *do*. It is made up of the same arrangement of whole and half steps as a major scale.

jazz An original American style of music that features swing rhythms, syncopation and improvisation.

jongleur [Fr.] An entertainer who traveled from town to town during medieval times, often telling stories and singing songs.

key Determined by a song's or scale's home tone, or keynote.

key signature A symbol or set of symbols that determines the key of a piece of music.

Eb major
C minor

ledger lines Short lines that appear above, between treble and bass clefs, or below the bass clef, used to expand the notation.

legato *(leh-GAH-toh)* [It.] A connected and sustained style of singing and playing.

lento *(LEN-toh)* [It.] Slow; a little faster than *largo*, a little slower than *adagio*.

lied *(leet)* [Ger.] A song in the German language, generally with a secular text.

liturgical text A text that has been written for the purpose of worship in a church setting.

lute An early form of the guitar.

Lydian scale *(LIH-dee-an)* [Gk.] A modal scale that starts and ends on *fa*.

lyrics The words of a song.

madrigal A poem that has been set to music in the language of the composer. Featuring several imitative parts, it usually has a secular text and is generally sung *a cappella*.

maestoso *(mah-eh-STOH-soh)* [It.] Perform majestically.

major chord A chord that can be based on the *do, mi,* and *sol* of a major scale.

major scale A scale that has *do* as its home tone, or keynote. It is made up of a specific arrangement of whole steps and half steps in the following order: W + W + H + W + W + W + H.

major tonality A song that is based on a major scale with *do* as its keynote, or home tone.

mangulina A traditional dance from the Dominican Republic.

marcato *(mar-CAH-toh)* [It.] A stressed and accented style of singing and playing.

mass A religious service of prayers and ceremonies originating in the Roman Catholic Church consisting of spoken and sung sections. It consists of several sections divided into two groups: proper (text changes for every day) and ordinary (text stays the same in every mass). Between the years 1400 and 1600, the mass assumed its present form consisting of the Kyrie, Gloria, Credo, Sanctus and Agnus Dei. It may include chants, hymns and psalms as well. The mass also developed into large musical works for chorus, soloists and even orchestra.

measure The space between two barlines.

Medieval period The historical period in Western civilization also known as the Middle Ages (400–1430).

medley A collection of songs musically linked together.

melisma (*muh-LIZ-mah*) [Gk.] A group of notes sung to a single syllable or word.

melismatic singing (*muh-liz-MAT-ik*) [Gk.] A style of text setting in which one syllable is sung over many notes.

melodic contour The overall shape of the melody.

melodic minor scale A minor scale that uses raised sixth and seventh notes: *fi* (raised from *fa*) and *si* (raised from *sol*). Often, these notes are raised in ascending patterns, but not in descending patterns.

melody A logical succession of musical tones.

meter A way of organizing rhythm.

meter signature *See* time signature.

metronome marking A sign that appears over the top line of the staff at the beginning of a piece or section of music that indicates the tempo. It shows the kind of note that will receive the beat and the number of beats per minute as measured by a metronome.

mezzo forte (*MEH-tsoh FOR tay*) [It.] A dynamic that indicates to sing or play medium loud. (*mf*)

mezzo piano (*MEH-tsoh pee-AH-noh*) [It.] A dynamic that indicates to sing or play medium soft. (*mp*)

mezzo voce (*MEH-tsoh VOH-cheh*) [It.] With half voice; reduced volume and tone.

minor chord A chord that can be based on the *la*, *do*, and *mi* of a minor scale.

minor scale A scale that has *la* as its home tone, or keynote. It is made up of a specific arrangement of whole steps and half steps in the following order: W + H +W + W + H + W + W.

minor tonality A song that is based on a minor scale with *la* as its keynote, or home tone.

mixed meter A technique in which the time signature or meter changes frequently within a piece of music.

Mixolydian scale (*mix-oh-LIH-dee-an*) [Gr.] A modal scale that starts and ends on *sol*.

modal scale A scale based on a mode. Like major and minor scales, each modal scale is made up of a specific arrangement of whole steps and half steps, with the half steps occurring between *mi* and *fa*, and *ti* and *do*.

mode An early system of pitch organization that was used before major and minor scales and keys were developed.

modulation A change in the key or tonal center of a piece of music within the same song.

molto [It.] Very or much; for example, *molto rit.* means "much slower."

motet (*moh-teht*) Originating as a Medieval and Renaissance polyphonic song, this choral form of composition became an unaccompanied work, often in contrapuntal style. Also, a short, sacred choral piece with a Latin text that is used in religious services but is not a part of the regular mass.

motive A shortened expression, sometimes contained within a phrase.

music critic A writer who gives an evaluation of a musical performance.

music notation Any means of writing down music, including the use of notes, rests and symbols.

musical A play or film whose action and dialogue are combined with singing and dancing.

musical theater An art form that combines acting, singing, and dancing to tell a story. It often includes staging, costumes, lighting and scenery.

mysterioso [It.] Perform in a mysterious or haunting way; to create a haunting mood.

N

narrative song A song that tells a story.

national anthem A patriotic song adopted by nations through tradition or decree.

nationalism Patriotism; pride of country. This feeling influenced many Romantic composers such as Wagner, Tchaikovsky, Dvořák, Chopin and Brahms.

natural A symbol that cancels a previous sharp or flat, or a sharp or flat in a key signature. (♮)

natural minor scale A minor scale that uses no altered pitches or accidentals.

no breath mark A direction not to take a breath at a specific place in the composition. (N.B.)

non troppo (*nahn TROH-poh*) [It.] Not too much; for example, *allegro non troppo*, "not too fast."

notation Written notes, symbols and directions used to represent music within a composition.

O

octave An interval of two pitches that are eight notes apart on a staff.

ode A poem written in honor of a special person or occasion. These poems were generally dedicated to a member of a royal family. In music, an ode usually includes several sections for choir, soloists and orchestra.

opera A combination of singing, instrumental music, dancing and drama that tells a story.

optional divisi (*opt.div.*) Indicating a split in the music into optional harmony, shown by a smaller cued note.

oral tradition Music that is learned through rote or by ear and is interpreted by its performer(s).

oratorio (*or-uh-TOR-ee-oh*) [It.] A dramatic work for solo voices, chorus and orchestra presented without theatrical action. Usually, oratorios are based on a literary or religious theme.

ostinato (*ahs-tuh-NAH-toh*) [It.] A rhythmic or melodic passage that is repeated continuosly.

overture A piece for orchestra that serves as an introduction to an opera or other dramatic work.

P

palate The roof of the mouth; the hard palate is at the front, the soft palate is at the back.

parallel motion A technique in which two or more melodic lines move in the same direction.

parallel sixths A group of intervals that are a sixth apart and which move at the same time and in the same direction.

parallel thirds A group of intervals that are a third apart and which move at the same time and in the same direction.

part-singing Two or more parts singing an independent melodic line at the same time.

patsch The act of slapping one's hands on one's thighs.

pentatonic scale A five-tone scale using the pitches *do, re, mi, sol* and *la*.

perfect fifth An interval of two pitches that are five notes apart on a staff.

perfect fourth An interval of two pitches that are four notes apart on a staff.

phrase A musical idea with a beginning and an end.

Phrygian scale (*FRIH-gee-an*) [Gk.] A modal scale that starts and ends on *mi*.

pianissimo (*pee-ah-NEE-see-moh*) [It.] A dynamic that indicates to sing or play very soft. (*pp*)

piano (*pee-AH-noh*) [It.] A dynamic that indicates to sing or play soft. (*p*)

pitch Sound, the result of vibration; the highness or lowness of a tone, determined by the number of vibrations per second.

pitch matching In a choral ensemble, the ability to sing the same notes as those around you.

piu (*pew*) [It.] More; for example, *piu forte* means "more loudly."

poco (*POH-koh*) [It.] Little; for example *poco dim.* means "a little softer."

poco a poco (*POH-koh ah POH-koh*) [It.] Little by little; for example, *poco a poco cresc.* means "little by little increase in volume."

polyphony (*pah-LIH-fun-nee*) [Gk.] Literally, "many sounding." A type of music in which there are two or more different melodic lines being sung or played at the same time. Polyphony was refined during the Renaissance, and this period is sometimes called "golden age of polyphony."

polyrhythms A technique in which several different rhythms are performed at the same time.

presto (*PREH-stoh*) [It.] Very fast.

program music A descriptive style of music composed to relate or illustrate a specific incident, situation or drama; the form of the piece is often dictated or influenced by the nonmusical program. This style commonly occurs in music composed during the Romantic period.

Q

quarter note A note that represents one beat of sound when the quarter note receives the beat.

quarter rest A rest that represents one beat of silence when the quarter note receives the beat.

quartet A group of four singers or instrumentalists.

R

rallentando (*rall.*) (*rahl-en-TAHN-doh*) [It.] Meaning to "perform more and more slowly." *See* ritard.

refrain A repeated section at the end of each phrase or verse in a song. Also known as a chorus.

register, vocal A term used for different parts of the singer's range, such as head register, or head voice (high notes); and chest register, or chest voice (low notes).

relative minor scale A minor scale that shares the same key signature as its corresponding major scale. Both scales share the same half steps, between *mi* and *fa,* and *ti* and *do.*

Renaissance period The historical period in Western civilization from 1430 to 1600.

repeat sign A symbol that indicates that a section of music should be repeated.

repetition The restatement of a musical idea; repeated pitches; repeated "A" section in ABA form.

requiem (*REK-wee-ehm*) [Lt.] Literally, "rest." A mass written and performed to honor the dead and comfort the living.

resonance Reinforcement and intensification of sound by vibration.

rest A symbol used in music notation to indicate silence.

rhythm The combination of long and short notes and rests in music. These may move with the beat, faster than the beat or slower than the beat.

ritard *(rit.)* *(ree-TAHRD)* [It.] A tempo marking that indicates to gradually get slower.

Romantic period The historical period in Western civilization from 1820 to 1900.

rondo form A form in which a repeated section is separated by several contrasting sections.

rote The act of learning a song by hearing it over and over again.

round *See* canon.

rubato *(roo-BAH-toh)* [It.] The freedom to slow down and/or speed up the tempo without changing the overall pulse of a piece of music.

S

sacred music Music associated with religious services or themes.

scale A group of pitches that are sung or played in succession and are based on a particular home tone, or keynote.

scat singing An improvisational style of singing that uses nonsense syllables instead of words. It was made popular by jazz trumpeter Louis Armstrong.

sea chantey A song sung by sailors, usually in rhythm with their work.

secular music Music not associated with religious services or themes.

sempre *(SEHM-preh)* [It.] Always, continually.

sempre accelerando *(sempre accel.)* *(SEHM-preh ahk-chel)* [It.] A term that indicates to gradually increase the tempo of a piece or section of music.

sequence A successive musical pattern that begins on a higher or lower pitch each time it is repeated.

serenata [It.] A large-scale musical work written in honor of a special occasion. Generally performed in the evening or outside, it is often based on a mythological theme.

sforzando *(sfohr-TSAHN-doh)* [It.] A sudden strong accent on a note or chord. (*sfz*)

sharp A symbol that raises the pitch of a given note one half step.

shekere An African shaker consisting of a hollow gourd surrounded by beads.

sight-sing Reading and singing music at first sight.

simile *(sim.)* *(SIM-ee-leh)* [It.] To continue the same way.

simple meter Any meter in which the quarter note receives the beat, and the division of the beat is based on two eighth notes. 2/4, 3/4 and 4/4 are examples of simple meter.

singing posture The way one sits or stands while singing.

sixteenth note A note that represents one quarter beat of sound when the quarter note receives the beat. Four sixteenth notes equal one beat of sound when the quarter note receives the beat.

sixteenth rest A rest that represents one quarter beat of silence when the quarter note receives the beat. Four sixteenth rests equal one beat of silence when the quarter note receives the beat.

skipwise motion The movement from a given note to another note that is two or more notes above or below it on the staff.

slur A curved line placed over or under a group of notes to indicate that they are to be performed without a break.

solfège syllables Pitch names using *do, re, mi, fa, sol, la, ti, do,* etc.

solo One person singing or playing an instrument alone.

sonata-allegro form A large ABA form consisting of three sections: exposition, development and recapitulation. This form was made popular during the Classical period.

soprano The highest-sounding female voice.

sostenuto *(SAHS-tuh-noot-oh)* [It.] The sustaining of a tone or the slackening of tempo.

sotto voce In a quiet, subdued manner; "under" the voice.

spirito *(SPEE-ree-toh)* [It.] Spirited; for example, *con spirito* ("with spirit").

spiritual Songs that were first sung by African American slaves, usually based on biblical themes or stories.

staccato *(stah-KAH-toh)* [It.] A short and detached style of singing or playing.

staff A series of five horizontal lines and four spaces on which notes are written. A staff is like a ladder. Notes placed higher on the staff sound higher than notes placed lower on the staff.

stage presence A performer's overall appearance on stage, including enthusiasm, facial expression and posture.

staggered breathing In ensemble singing, the practice of planning breaths so that no two singers take a breath at the same time, thus creating the overall effect of continuous singing.

staggered entrances A technique in which different parts and voices enter at different times.

stanza A section in a song in which the words change on each repeat. Also known as a verse.

stepwise motion The movement from a given note to another note that is directly above or below it on the staff.

strophe A verse or stanza in a song.

strophic A form in which the melody repeats while the words change from verse to verse.

style The particular character of a musical work; often indicated by words at the beginning of a composition, telling the performer the general manner in which the piece is to be performed.

subdominant chord A chord built on the fourth note of a scale. In a major scale, this chord uses the notes *fa, la* and *do,* and it may be called the **IV** ("four") chord, since it is based on the fourth note of the major scale, or *fa.* In a minor scale, this chord uses the notes *re, fa* and *la,* and it may be called the **iv** ("four") chord, since it is based on the fourth note of the minor scale, or *re.*

subito (sub.) *(SOO-bee-toh)* [It.] Suddenly.

suspension The holding over of one or more musical tones in a chord into the following chord, producing a momentary discord.

swing rhythms Rhythms in which the second eighth note of each beat is played or sung like the last third of triplet, creating an uneven, "swing" feel. A style often found in jazz and blues. Swing rhythms are usually indicated at the beginning of a song or section.

syllabic *See* syllabic singing.

syllabic singing A style of text setting in which one syllable is sung on each note.

syllabic stress The stressing of one syllable over another.

symphonic poem A single-movement work for orchestra, inspired by a painting, play or other literary or visual work. Franz Liszt was a prominent composer of symphonic poems. Also known as a tone poem.

symphony A large-scale work for orchestra.

syncopation The placement of accents on a weak beat or a weak portion of the beat, or on a note or notes that normally do not receive extra emphasis.

synthesizer A musical instrument that produces sounds electronically, rather than by the physical vibrations of an acoustic instrument.

tempo   Terms in music that indicate how fast or slow to sing or play.

tempo I or tempo primo   *See* a tempo.

tenor   The highest-sounding male voice.

tenuto *(teh-NOO-toh)*   [It.] A symbol placed above or below a given note indicating that the note should receive stress and/or that its value should be slightly extended. (🎵)

text   Words, usually set in a poetic style, that express a central thought, idea or narrative.

texture   The thickness of the different layers of horizontal and vertical sounds.

theme   A musical idea, usually a melody.

theme and variation form   A musical form in which variations of the basic theme make up the composition.

third   An interval of two pitches that are three notes apart on a staff.

tie   A curved line used to connect two or more notes of the same pitch together in order to make one longer note. (🎵)

tied notes   Two or more notes of the same pitch connected together with a tie in order to make one longer note.

timbre   The tone quality of a person's voice or musical instrument.

time signature   The set of numbers at the beginning of a piece of music. The top number indicates the number of beats per measure. The bottom number indicates the kind of note that receives the beat. Time signature is sometimes called meter signature.

to coda   Skip to (⊕) or CODA.

tone color   That which distinguishes the voice or tone of one singer or instrument from another; for example, a soprano from an alto, or a flute from a clarinet. *See* timbre.

tonic chord   A chord built on the home tone, or keynote of a scale. In a major scale, this chord uses the notes *do, mi* and *sol*, and it may be called the **I** ("one") chord, since it is based on the first note of the major scale, or *do*. In a minor scale, this chord uses the notes *la, do* and *mi*, and it may be called the **i** ("one") chord, since it is based on the first note of the minor scale, or *la*.

treble clef   A clef that generally indicates notes that sound higher than middle C.

trio   A group of three singers or instrumentalists with usually one on a part.

triplet   A group of notes in which three notes of equal duration are sung in the time normally given to two notes of equal duration.

troppo *(TROHP-oh)*   [It.] Too much; for example, *allegro non troppo* ("not too fast").

tutti *(TOO-tee)*   [It.] Meaning "all" or "together."

twelve-tone music   A type of music that uses all twelve tones of the scale equally. Developed in the early twentieth century, Arnold Schoenberg is considered to be the pioneer of this style of music.

two-part music   A type of music in which two different parts are sung or played.

unison   All parts singing or playing the same notes at the same time.

variation   A modification of a musical idea, usually after its initial appearance in a piece.

vivace *(vee-VAH-chay)*   [It.] Very fast; lively.

vocal jazz   A popular style of music characterized by strong prominent meter, improvisation and dotted or syncopated patterns. Sometimes sung *a cappella*.

W

whole note A note that represents four beats of sound when the quarter note receives the beat. o

whole rest A rest that represents four beats of silence when the quarter note receives the beat. ▬

whole step The combination of two successive half steps.

word painting A technique in which the music reflects the meaning of the words.

word stress The act of singing important parts of the text in a more accented style than the other parts.

Y

yoik A vocal tradition of the Sámi people of the Arctic region of Sampi that features short melodic phrases that are repeated with slight variations.

Classified Index

A Cappella

The Battle Cry Of Freedom 122

Festival Procession 34

Leave Her, Johnny 170

Now Is The Month Of Maying 66

Red River Valley 22

Sing To The Lord 212

Soldier's Hallelujah 42

Composers

Thomas Morley (1557–1602)
Now Is The Month Of Maying 66

Johann Sebastian Bach (1685–1750)
Der Herr segne euch 74

Wolfgang Amadeus Mozart (1756–1791)
Ave Verum Corpus 86

George Frederick Root (1825–1895)
The Battle Cry Of Freedom 122

Teodoro Cottrau (1827–1879)
Santa Lucia 206

Johannes Brahms (1833–1897)
Da unten im Tale 94

Bob Chilcott (b. 1955)
Be Cool 14

Folk

African American Spiritual
Joshua! (Fit The Battle Of Jericho) . . 158

New River Train 174

The Shepherd's Spiritual 56

American
Frog Went A-Courtin' 140

Pretty Saro 198

Red River Valley 22

Cuban
Guantanamera 152

German
Da unten im Tale 94

Foreign Language

German
Da unten im Tale 94

Der Herr segne euch 74

Italian
Santa Lucia 206

Latin
Ave Verum Corpus 86

Festival Procession 34

Spanish
Guantanamera 152

Instruments

Percussion
Festival Procession 34

Frog Went A-Courtin' 140

Soldier's Hallelujah 42

Music & History

Medieval
Festival Procession 34

Renaissance
Now Is The Month Of Maying 66

You Gentlemen Of England 218

Baroque
Der Herr segne euch 74

Classical
Ave Verum Corpus 86

Romantic
The Battle Cry Of Freedom 122

Da unten im Tale 94

Santa Lucia 206

Contemporary
Be Cool 14

Poetry

Come Travel With Me 128

Guantanamera 152

Sea Chantey

Codfish Shanty 26

Leave Her, Johnny 170

On The Deep, Blue Sea 184

Seasonal, Patriotic

The Battle Cry Of Freedom 122

Festival Procession 34

Light The Candles Of Hanukkah . . . 48

Now Is The Month Of Maying 66

This Land Is Your Land 2

The Shepherd's Spiritual 56

Soldier's Hallelujah 42

Vocal Jazz

Be Cool 14

Joshua! (Fit The Battle Of Jericho) . . 158

Listening Selections

As Vesta Was Descending
Thomas Weelkes 103

"Three Voltas" from *Terpsichore*
Michael Praetorius 103

"Gloria in excelsis Deo"
from *Gloria in D Major*
Antonio Vivaldi 107

"The Arrival of the Queen of Sheba"
from *Solomon*
George Frideric Handel 107

"The Heavens Are Telling"
from *Creation*
Franz Joseph Haydn 111

Eine Kleine Nachtmusik, First Movement
Wolfgang Amadeus Mozart 111

"Toreador Chorus" from *Carmen*
Georges Bizet 115

The Moldau (excerpt)
Bedrich Smetana 115

The Battle of Jericho
arr. Moses Hogan 119

"Infernal Dance of King Kaschei"
from *The Firebird*
Igor Stravinsky 119

Index of Songs
and Spotlights

Ave Verum Corpus 86
The Battle Cry Of Freedom 122
Be Cool 14
Codfish Shanty 26
Come Travel With Me 128
Da unten im Tale 94
Der Herr segne euch 74
Festival Procession 34
Frog Went A-Courtin' 140
Guantanamera 152
Joshua! (Fit The Battle Of Jericho) 158
Leave Her, Johnny 170
Light The Candles Of Hanukkah 48
New River Train 174
Now Is The Month Of Maying 66
On The Deep, Blue Sea 184
Pretty Saro 198
Red River Valley 22
Santa Lucia 206
Sing To The Lord 212
Soldier's Hallelujah 42
The Shepherd's Spiritual 56
This Land Is Your Land 2
You Gentlemen Of England 218

Spotlights

Arranging 21
Breath Management 169
Careers In Music 127
Changing Voice 197
Concert Etiquette 139
Diction 120
Improvisation 183
Posture 13
Vocal Production 217
Vowels 65

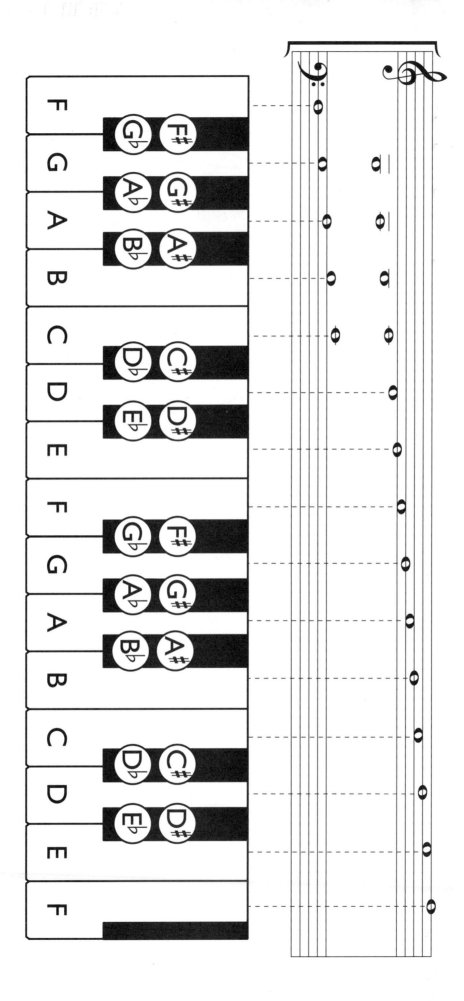